A CELEBRATION OF THE ⭐ American Girl STORY

★ American Girl®
ULTIMATE VISUAL GUIDE

WRITTEN BY CARRIE ANTON, LAURIE CALKHOVEN, AND ERIN FALLIGANT

Contents

Foreword

A girl and her doll

How a girl relates to her doll is a marvelous mystery. She can be her doll's mother or her best friend. Sometimes she is the doll herself—becoming part of her world and her time, standing in her shoes, facing her challenges, and feeling her sadness and her joy.

This beautiful book welcomes you into the charming world of American Girl® dolls. Since their introduction in 1986, the dolls have been the beloved companions of millions of girls. On their sturdy little shoulders, American Girl dolls have carried the wishes, dreams, and make-believe adventures of the girls who play with them.

The dolls enable girls to lift the stories about the American Girl characters right up off the pages of the books and make up adventures for them on their own. The dolls help a girl make friends with the characters who lived long ago and far away, or in circumstances very different from her own.

It has been my life's privilege and honor to tell the stories of many of the American Girls. I wrote about the historical characters; first Molly, then Samantha, Felicity, Josefina, Kit, and Maryellen. I've written about their best friends, too: Emily, Nellie, Elizabeth, and Ruthie. I have seen first-hand how girls love their dolls. I've seen dolls handed down from mother to daughter—some dolls perfectly preserved, and some with tangled, lovingly brushed hair—but all deeply, deeply treasured.

Walk into the world of American Girl shown to you on these pages. Read about how carefully every enchanting dress, accessory, or piece of furniture was researched, planned, and delivered to loving girls. As you immerse yourself, you'll be delighted, inspired, encouraged, educated, and changed—just as millions of American girls have been before you.

Valerie Tripp

Meet American Girl

It began with a dream

On a visit to Colonial Williamsburg in the early 1980s, Pleasant T. Rowland had a visionary idea. Inspired by the history she saw coming to life around her, Pleasant decided to publish a line of books that fed a girl's imagination and taught history through the lives of its young heroines. To accompany the books, she would create beautifully detailed dolls and accessories that inspired a girl to act out the stories and give her the experience of touching the past. Nothing like this had ever been done before, but that didn't stop Pleasant from daring to make her dream come true.

The original books

Kirsten Larson™
1854

Samantha Parkington™
1904

Molly McIntire™
1944

Stories of the past

The books were written to show how girls' lives changed across time, but also, in many ways, stayed the same.

History for girls

Pleasant started by creating The American Girls Collection, featuring three strong, smart, compassionate characters—nine-year-old girls growing up at different times in America's past. She created dolls for the characters with a series of three books for each one.

"From the beginning, I knew we had to build a publishing company, a doll company, a toy company, a clothing company and a direct mail company all at once. But what we were really building was a 'girl company,' and anything that was good for girls was ours to give them."

Pleasant T. Rowland, Founder

> *"The books are the heart of The American Girls Collection. The stories of the American Girls' lives, simple on the surface but rich and rewarding in their emotional truth, will stay with a girl for years to come. That is the nourishment, the goodness, that will strengthen her spirit and guide her. That goodness has the power to change her and, through her, change the world."*
>
> *Pleasant T. Rowland, Founder*

Illustration and product sketches from *Kirsten Learns a Lesson*

Photo essay from *Kirsten Learns a Lesson*

Product sketches and illustration from *Samantha Learns a Lesson*

Illustration and product sketches from *Happy Birthday, Molly!*

Pleasant T. Rowland

Books and collections

Rich illustrations and a photo essay at the end of the original books let girls peek into the past and see what girls' worlds looked like long ago. Collections of outfits and accessories for the dolls were developed along with the beautiful book illustrations. The original sketches above show just some of the products developed for the characters.

A girl company grows

Thirty years later, Pleasant's dream has come true, in ways far bigger than she had ever imagined. 135 million books and nearly 20 million dolls are in the hands and hearts of girls all over the world. The generation of girls who first fell in love with the American Girl characters now have daughters of their own. Who knows what bold, new ideas they will dream up?

Stories and style

From the very beginning, the unique combination of American Girl® books and dolls have made them stand out from the crowd. From the first historical characters to the latest Girl of the Year™, their stories and style have brought these one-of-a-kind dolls to life.

The dolls are easy to pose for play.

A German dollmaker

A doll made by Götz, a German doll company, provided the inspiration for the look of every American Girl. Götz made the original American Girl dolls, and the same face mold is still used today.

The design of the original dolls, including Samantha, was inspired by a German-made doll.

Huggable dolls

The dolls are made to be lovable and durable—to last for many years. The 18-inch dolls have soft bodies, but their arms and legs are made of sturdy vinyl so that they can pose, sit, and stand.

Dolls and books

All of the original characters came with a book. Every American Girl doll has a story that encourages girls to imagine different times and places, and explore what makes them unique.

Felicity in her original Meet dress with the book Meet Felicity

Kaya™ 1764

Julie Albright™ 1974

BeForever™

The historical line was renamed BeForever in 2014. A total of 20 dolls, including friend dolls, have been introduced since 1986. The BeForever line spans more than 200 years of American history—from Kaya, a Native American growing up in 1764, to Julie, a girl coping with change in 1974.

Lea Clark™
2016

Truly Me™

The American Girl of Today debuted in 1995 to show girls that they're a part of history, too. Girls could select from 20 combinations of hair, skin, and eye colors. Now, as Truly Me, there are 40 combinations available for girls to choose from.

Girl of the Year™

Since 2001, American Girl has also introduced over a dozen Girl of the Year dolls. The characters share the same interests and challenges as today's girls and inspire them to dream big. Since 2005, a new Girl of the Year has been released annually.

Lindsey Bergman™ 2001

One of the original American Girl of Today dolls

Design time

In the book Grace Stirs it Up!, Grace learns to bake macarons.

Creating a new American Girl® doll takes time—up to two years for a Girl of the Year™, and as many as three years for a BeForever™ character. Researchers, editors, and designers work together to come up with each girl's story. As the story and designs develop, the character's personality starts to shine through.

Teamwork and travel

Authors and editors work with experts to come up with true-to-life stories. Mary Casanova, the author of the Grace series, explored Paris and met with a French baker who taught her how to bake macarons—just like Grace does in the story.

Did you know?

The American Girl team might discuss 100 doll names before choosing just one. The name has to fit her personality and, for the BeForever characters, be culturally accurate for her time period, too.

Hairstyles tested for Maryellen

Doll details

While the story is being developed, the doll is, too. Every feature is a big decision, from the doll's skin and eye color to the style of her hair. Designers try out many hairstyles before choosing the perfect one.

Maryellen's final hairstyle

McKenna's early color palette (above), and the outfit it inspired (right)

Color play

Predicting fashions that will be popular when the next Girl of the Year comes out isn't easy. Designers keep an eye on trends, and collect fabric and color swatches. They create a color palette for each character before designing her outfits.

Saige's blue dress (center) was the winning outfit.

Testing, testing

For help in choosing outfits, American Girl sometimes calls on the real experts: girls and their moms. In an online survey, girls rated three outfits for Saige, the Girl of the Year in 2013. They helped choose Saige's final Meet outfit.

Samantha's final Buster Brown school outfit

Early sketch of Samantha's school outfit

Outfit inspiration

To study outfits from the past, researchers and designers visit museums and read old books and magazines. Samantha's Buster Brown school dress was inspired by a fashion magazine from the early 1900s.

Cool accessories

For Truly Me™ accessories, designers look to the activities and products that girls love today. In 2009, that was sneakers with built-in wheels!

Creating Kaya™

Developing Kaya, a Native American character, took extra time and care. American Girl spent five years researching and creating her world. Kaya's stories are set in 1764 to show that America's history began long before the Revolution. One of the reasons the Nez Perce tribe was chosen is because many members still live near their homeland today.

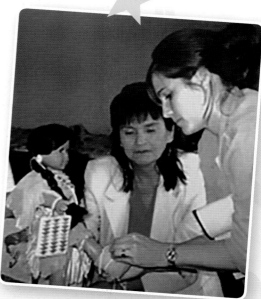

Showing Kaya to a member of the research group.

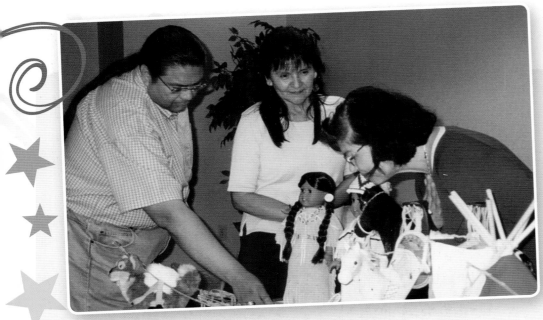

Members of the advisory board reviewing Kaya's product.

Asking the experts

American Girl asked the Nez Perce for permission and help in telling Kaya's story. A group of tribal elders, educators, and historians reviewed Kaya's stories as well as every detail of her entire collection, from hair ties to moccasins.

Kaya's homeland

The Nez Perce live in Idaho, Washington, and Oregon. A team from American Girl visited the area to eat traditional foods, listen to legends, and see some of the important places in Nez Perce history and culture.

The team visited the area to get a feel for the landscape Kaya would have lived in.

An illustration from one of Kaya's books, inspired by her unique name.

A decorated Nez Perce rawhide parfleche.

One-of-a-kind name

Most BeForever™ dolls are given popular names from the past, but Nez Perce children never share a name—each is unique. Instead of borrowing a name, the team created one: Kaya'aton'my' [ky-YAAH-aton-my], or "she who arranges rocks." In the story, Kaya's mother named her for the first thing she saw after her birth—a woman arranging stones for a ceremonial lodge. She hoped the name would give Kaya the woman's wisdom and strength.

Trip to the past

American Girl researchers and designers visited museums to look at Nez Perce items from long ago. Kaya's accessories, such as her painted parfleche (bag), are designed to look authentic to her time.

Colorful Nez Perce designs decorate Kaya's parfleche.

Detailed sketch of Kaya's product

Kaya is the only doll with a closed-mouth smile.

Early jingle dress sketch

Special smile

The product development team worked closely with the advisory board to develop a new and special mold for Kaya. Her slightly rounded face, short straight nose, and soft smile reflect Kaya's gentle nature.

A dress for today

In the 1760s, girls like Kaya didn't own many outfits so her collection is different from other BeForever dolls. Designers made Kaya something special: a modern jingle dress that Nez Perce girls might wear to a pow-wow today.

Kaya's final jingle dress

Packaged with care

Pleasant's original sketch of the doll box

A box is born

In Pleasant T. Rowland's early sketch, the American Girl box was square and had a window so girls could see the doll sitting inside. In the end, a rectangular box was designed because the dolls are better protected while standing.

From the very beginning, American Girl® dolls, outfits, and accessories have been packaged with care. As girls slid the satin ribbon off the first burgundy box, they knew there was something special inside.

Original Pleasant Company boxes

The original boxes

The first boxes were burgundy, tied with white satin ribbon, and decorated with a sticker of the Pleasant Company logo.

A garment bag for an early outfit

THE AMERICAN GIRLS COLLECTION®

Outfits

A beautiful dress deserved its own garment bag and hanger. Certain outfits were shipped in bags until around 2000, when all outfits came in boxes.

First Pleasant Company logo

First logo

The logo's design evoked the historical art form of the silhouette. It served as a reminder that books and dolls are timeless pastimes that have provided girls with "Pleasant Company" for generations.

Changes over time

Since 1986, the design of the logo has changed many times. Customers were responsible for the change from Pleasant Company to American Girl—a name they felt was a better fit for the brand they loved.

1986   1996   2006   2016

Kit was added to the logo design in 2000.

American girls

In 1995, the packaging was updated to show all of the dolls. This meant the design had to be updated every time a new doll was released. It became difficult to keep up with. The last design of this style includes Kit, the new American Girl doll in 2000.

BeForever™   *Girl of the Year™*   *Truly Me™*

A look for each line

BeForever, Girl of the Year, and Truly Me doll boxes now have their own colors, logos, and patterns.

Doll Hospital

When accidents happen, experts from the American Girl® Doll Hospital are standing by. They help with everything from a thorough cleaning to more serious repair jobs, such as a part replacement. When a girl admits her doll to the hospital, the doll is examined from head to toe by doll doctors. After receiving treatment, the doll is sent home in perfect condition.

Before and after

The Doll Hospital has a cure for every patient, whatever her ailment! Whether a doll needs her hair detangled, skin cleaned, or a limb replaced, the doll doctors at the hospital can fix her up.

Doll upon admission

Doll after receiving treatment

Additional services

The Doll Hospital provides Wellness Visits for dolls that need cleaning, hair brushing, and ear piercing. Dolls can also be admitted to have hearing aids fitted.

Doll with hearing aid fitted

Special care

Before a doll is discharged, Doll Hospital experts brush her hair and clean her skin. Dolls leave the hospital with a Certificate of Good Health, a get-well-soon card, a hospital gown, and an ID bracelet.

Did you know?

Following an employee suggestion, doll repairs have been offered since 1988. By the end of 2015, nearly 760,000 dolls had been cared for at the Doll Hospital.

☆ **American Girl**
DOLL HOSPITAL

Certificate of Good Health
I hereby certify that

_____
is now ready to return home and resume all regular activities slowly. I prescribe plenty of rest for one week, plus an extra-strength dose of TLC (tender loving care) to be administered at least twice daily.

_____
Doctor-in-charge
American Girl Doll Hospital

30 years of American Girl

1984

★ In Pleasant's early sketches, she considers naming the company "Pleasantries" before deciding on Pleasant Company.

1985

★ Pleasant Company opens its first office in a converted warehouse on Blount Street in Madison, Wisconsin.

1987

★ The first birthday sets are released.
★ A special catalogue is distributed to schools and libraries around the country.

1987

*Samantha's dresses were made by Jessie, the seamstress, who found out about the latest fashions by reading **Delineator**, a magazine for ladies at the turn of the century. Pleasant Company's designers pored over rare editions of **Delineator**, too. Pictures like this one gave us our inspiration for the Samantha dresses we designed for you.*

Images from historic fashion magazines, like the one pictured here, were just one source of inspiration for the design of the girls' outfits.

★ The first American Girls Wardrobe collection lets girls dress like Samantha, Kirsten, and Molly.

American Girl has been inspiring girls of all ages for more than 30 years with its beautiful dolls and their unforgettable stories and charming collections. This timeline features key moments in the history of American Girl®—from founder Pleasant T. Rowland's first ideas to the wide variety of books, dolls, and playthings available today.

Pleasant T. Rowland poses with the inaugural American Girl dolls and their collections, including beds and storage trunks.

1986

★ The first three American Girl dolls, Kirsten Larson™, Samantha Parkington™, and Molly McIntire™ debut.

★ 500,000 girls and their families across the country receive copies of Pleasant Company catalogue.

Kirsten in her summer outfit

Kirsten in her winter outfit

1988

1988–1989

★ The first summer and winter collections debut for Kirsten, Samantha, and Molly.
★ The American Girl Doll Hospital opens.

★ Pleasant Company moves to its current offices in Middleton, Wisconsin.

1990

Samantha's desk

★ Samantha, Kirsten, and Molly's school desks are released.

1993

The first book in Addy's series

MEET ADDY
AN AMERICAN GIRL
~BOOK ONE~

THE AMERICAN GIRLS COLLECTION®

★ Historical character Addy Walker™ debuts. Her story is set in the Civil War era.
★ One million American Girl dolls have been sold!

1996

American Girl is going on-line!
Starting May 1, 1996, look for our new site on the World Wide Web. Here's the address: http://www.pleasantco.com Come visit us on-line, and help dream up future issues of AG! ★

AmericanGirl

1997

★ In May, the American Girl website launches with online features from *American Girl* magazine. Two months later, the *American Girls Club* debuts online along with information about events and how to request a catalogue.

★ Historical character Josefina Montoya™ is introduced. Her story is set in 19th century New Mexico.

1991

★ Felicity Merriman™, whose story is set in colonial America, debuts.

1992

★ The premier issue of *American Girl* magazine is mailed to girls around the country. It is the story of girls' lives today, and later gives inspiration to a new line of dolls called American Girl of Today.

1994

★ The first working accessory is released. Girls can churn real ice cream in Addy's Ice Cream Freezer.

1995

★ Pleasant Company introduces American Girl of Today, a line of dolls with contemporary clothing and accessories. Girls can choose from 20 dolls with five different eye colors, six hair colors, and three skin tones.

1998

The first American Girl Place opens at 111 E. Chicago Avenue.

1999

★ Pleasant Company's first flagship retail store, American Girl Place, opens in Chicago, Illinois.
★ Mattel acquires Pleasant Company.
★ American Girl of Today is renamed American Girl Today.

★ The first holiday "wishbook" catalogue is mailed to homes around the country.
★ The company's website, www.americangirl.com, is open for business.

2000

Coconut the Puppy

★ Coconut™ the Puppy debuts.
★ Historical character Kit Kittredge™ is introduced. Her story takes place during the Great Depression.
★ Pleasant T. Rowland retires.

Kit wearing her original Meet outfit.

2001

Lindsey's accessories, including a scooter, reflect the popular items girls had in the year 2001.

★ Lindsey Bergman™ debuts as the first contemporary character.

2004

★ Samantha's best friend, Nellie O'Malley™, debuts.
★ The first American Girl movie, *Samantha: An American Girl Holiday*, airs on TV.
★ Pleasant Company is renamed American Girl.

2005

★ American Girl renames the line of contemporary characters Girl of the Year™, with dancer Marisol Luna™.

2007

Nicki Fleming

★ Historical characters Julie Albright™ and Ivy Ling™ debut together. Their stories are set in 1970s San Francisco.
★ Animal lover Nicki Fleming™ is introduced as the Girl of the Year.

2008

Mia's ice skates

★ Figure skater Mia St. Clair™ is released as the Girl of the Year.
★ *Kit Kittredge: An American Girl* debuts in theaters nationwide.
★ Girls can now choose to have their dolls' ears pierced.

2002

★ Historical character Kaya™, a Nez Perce Indian, debuts.

2003

American Girl magazine is 10 years old.

Be on the Cover of AG! Contest Details Inside

American Girl

Throw a Pal Party

Take a Fun Friendship Quiz

Make Cards that Sparkle

It's AG's 10th Birthday!

Kailey Hopkins loves the ocean.

Kailey

★ *American Girl* magazine celebrates its 10th anniversary.
★ Contemporary character Kailey Hopkins™ makes her debut.
★ American Girl Place opens in New York City.

2005

Very Funny, Elizabeth!

★ Elizabeth Cole™, Felicity's best friend, is introduced.
★ American Girl Today is renamed Just Like You.
★ *Felicity: An American Girl Adventure* airs on TV.

2006

Jess McConnell

Emily Bennett

★ The Girl of the Year, adventurous Jess McConnell™, is released.
★ Emily Bennett™, Molly's English friend, is introduced.
★ *Molly: An American Girl on the Home Front* airs on TV.
★ American Girl Place opens in Los Angeles, California.

2009

Sonali, Chrissa, and Gwen

Rebecca's original accessories

Meet Rebecca

★ Chrissa Maxwell™, the Girl of the Year, is released with two best friend dolls, Sonali Matthews™ and Gwen Thompson™.
★ Historical character Rebecca Rubin™, a Jewish girl growing up in the early 1900s, debuts.
★ The first Girl of the Year movie, *An American Girl: Chrissa Stands Strong*, is released.

2010

★ Nature lover Lanie Holland™ debuts
as the Girl of the Year™.

★ Just Like You is renamed My American Girl.

Caroline Abbott sets sail
on the *Miss Caroline*.

2012

★ Girl of the Year, aspiring gymnast
McKenna Brooks™, is released.

★ The first American Girl direct-to-DVD movie, *An
American Girl: McKenna Shoots for the Stars,* launches.

★ Historical character Caroline Abbott™ debuts.
Her story takes place during the War of 1812.

Beforever™

Samantha
Parkington

Grace Thomas

truly me™

2014

Isabelle Palmer

★ Isabelle Palmer™, ballerina and costume designer,
debuts as the Girl of the Year.

★ The Historical line is renamed BeForever™.

★ Samantha is relaunched with new
clothes and accessories.

★ Three specialty boutiques open in Canada.

2015

★ Budding baker Grace Thomas™
debuts as the Girl of the Year.

★ Historical character Maryellen Larkin™ is
introduced. Her story is set in the 1950s.

★ My American Girl is renamed Truly Me™.

★ American Girl launches in Mexico.

2011

★ Native Hawaiian Kanani Akina™ makes her debut as the Girl of the Year.
★ American Girl celebrates its 25th anniversary!

2011

★ Historical characters Marie-Grace Gardner™ and Cécile Rey™ debut. Their stories are set in 1850s New Orleans.

2013

★ Artist Saige Copeland™ is released as the Girl of the Year.
★ American Girl mails its first catalogues to customers in Canada.

Maryellen Larkin

Lea Clark

Melody Ellison

2016

★ Jungle explorer Lea Clark™ is released as the Girl of the Year.
★ Historical character Melody Ellison™ debuts. Her story is set during the civil rights movement of the 1960s.

Kaya™ 1764 Felicity Merriman™ 1774 Elizabeth Cole™ 1775 Caroline Abbott™ 1812 Josefina Montoya™ 1824

Nellie O'Malley™ 1906 Rebecca Rubin™ 1914 Kit Kittredge™ 1934 Ruthie Smithens™ 1932 Molly McIntire™ 1944

Marie-Grace Gardner™ 1853   Cécile Rey™ 1853   Kirsten Larson™ 1854   Addy Walker™ 1864   Samantha Parkington™ 1904

BeForever™

Emily Bennett™ 1944   Maryellen Larkin™ 1954   Melody Ellison™ 1964   Julie Albright™ 1974   Ivy Ling™ 1976

Through the BeForever characters, girls today can find out what it would have been like to grow up during key moments in America's past. Each character's timeless story encourages modern girls to follow their hopes and dreams, and to draw inspiration from the past to build a better tomorrow.

Inspiring times

The BeForever characters overcome hard times with hope and determination. No matter what challenges they face, the characters dream big, and inspire girls today to do the same.

Fighting for the future

The characters' stories span more than 200 years from 1764 to the 1970s. Whatever the era, the stories always look to the future. Each BeForever character follows her heart, often making difficult decisions to improve her world and help create a brighter future for everyone.

Josefina's horno (oven)

Bringing history to life

Each BeForever character comes to life with historically accurate accessories. Their collections create a fun connection to times gone by. It's easy to imagine Josefina baking bread in an 18th century outdoor oven or to picture Felicity attending a ball dressed in the latest colonial fashions.

Left: Kit; Right: Melody

Kaya

NAME
Kaya'aton'my'

BIRTH YEAR
1754

HOMELAND
The Pacific Northwest

BIGGEST DREAM
To be a leader for her people

FAMILY
Mother, Father, Wing Feather and Sparrow (brothers), Speaking Rain and Brown Deer (sisters)

Kaya™ *1764*

Kaya is a courageous Nez Perce girl who dreams of being a leader for her people. Kaya's thirst for adventure and her desire to prove herself often lead her into trouble. Luckily, Kaya gains the patience she needs to stick to the right path.

The great outdoors

Amazing surprises can be found everywhere in nature, and Kaya loves living right in the middle of it all. When the tribe travels in search of food, Kaya brings her very own shelter called a tepee with her.

Furry friend

When it's time to move to a new campsite, Kaya attaches a travois to her dog, Tatlo. The sled, which is made of poles, carries light loads during the tribe's journey. Tatlo is always happy to help Kaya.

Saddle
pad

Sparks
Flying

Fringed
blanket

Small pouch
holds Kaya's
little treasures

Animal lover

Kaya loves horses—especially
Steps High, her Appaloosa mare.
Kaya is excited when Steps High
has a cute spotted foal. Kaya shows
courage when she rescues the
baby horse from a burning forest.
She names him Sparks Flying.

Cradleboard

KAYA'S DOLL

Kaya keeps her doll
snug and secure in
a cradleboard. Kaya
hangs it from her saddle
when she goes riding.

Moccasins

Winter home

With winter approaching, Kaya and her tribe will travel to longhouses. These permanent shelters, made from poles and covered with tule mats and hides, protect Kaya and her family from the winter weather. Kaya and her family will stay in a cozy longhouse until spring arrives. Before they pack up and travel to their winter homes, Kaya helps the tribe prepare for the journey.

Moveable shelter

Tepees provide shelter for Kaya and the Nez Perce tribe. Tepees are easy to pack and move, as Kaya's family does each season in order to gather food.

BEHIND THE SCENES

American Girl researchers and designers worked with a Nez Perce advisory panel and other experts while designing Kaya's tepee. They learned how to set up life-size versions.

Poles support the tepee

WILDLIFE
Kaya loves spotting wild animals. Just like the Nez Perce, this bear will settle into a cozy home for the winter.

Fire pit

Teatime

Like many colonial girls, Felicity has lessons on the proper way to serve tea to guests. Even though she would rather wear breeches and ride horses, Felicity must wear a pretty dress for her lessons.

Felicity
Merriman™ 1774

Growing up just before the start of the American Revolution, girls are expected to act like young ladies. But free-spirited Felicity would much rather spend time outdoors or in her father's shop. The war that breaks out between the United States and Great Britain teaches Felicity about courage, and what it means to be truly independent.

Canopy

Nightcap

Traditional colonial check curtains

SERVING SET

Felicity practices serving tea with an exquisite tea set. The pretty pink dishes are decorated with a popular lotus flower pattern.

Creamer

Tea caddy

Teapot

Tea tray

Sugar bowl

Cup and saucer

Beautiful bed

Felicity sleeps in a canopy bed that has four tall posts. On cold nights, Felicity draws her elegant bed hangings closed. The curtains shut out the chilly air.

Mob cap

Flower choker

Floral drawstring purse

Invitation

Felicity is thrilled to recieve an invitation to a dance lesson at the Governor's Palace. She has never been to a ball before, and Felicity knows she must behave like a lady for the occasion.

Invitation

NEW DRESS

Felicity sees this doll in a shop, and the dress catches her eye. Mother makes one just like it for Felicity to wear to her dance lesson.

Did you know?

Fashion dolls, like the one Felicity spots in the shop, showed colonial women what the stylish ladies in England were wearing. Then colonists could copy the latest fashions.

MEET
Felicity

NAME
Felicity Merriman

BIRTH YEAR
1765

HOMETOWN
Williamsburg, Virginia

BIGGEST DREAM
To stand up for what she believes in

FAMILY
Mother, Father,
Nan and Polly (sisters),
William (brother),
Grandfather

Saddle up

Horses require a lot of time and attention, including hauling heavy buckets of water and wheeling in big bales of hay. But for Felicity, looking after Penny and her foal, Patriot, is no chore. Felicity loves caring for her horses—and riding them, of course!

Posie

Felicity adores the sweet lamb Grandfather brings when he visits. Felicity names her Posie after the pretty spring flowers she sometimes frolicks through.

WHEELED IN

Felicity uses a wheelbarrow to help her carry heavy loads, including hay and bags of food, to the stables.

Penny

Patriot

Water bucket

Felicity's riding habit

41

Elizabeth
Cole™ *1775*

Elizabeth feels out of place when her family moves to Virginia from England. Her family is loyal to England during the war, and many other colonists are not. Even though Elizabeth and Felicity's families have different opinions about the American Revolution, the two girls remain great friends through it all.

Felicity's lacy cap

Elizabeth's summer dress

ROYAL DOLL
Elizabeth names her wooden doll Charlotte, after the King of England's wife.

Ball gown

At the party for her older sister's engagement, Elizabeth dances in a coral-and-pink ball gown. With her best friend Felicity by her side, Elizabeth has a wonderful time!

Did you know?
In colonial times, women and girls always covered their heads with hats, veils, or caps, such as the lace pinner cap Elizabeth wears to her sister's party.

MEET
Elizabeth

NAME
Elizabeth Cole

BIRTH YEAR
1765

HOMETOWN
Williamsburg, Virginia

BIGGEST DREAM
To hold love and loyalty in her heart

FAMILY
Mother, Father,
Annabelle (sister)

NOAH'S ARK

Elizabeth loves playing with Felicity's Noah's Ark toy. The Merrimans only take the toy out during the Christmas season.

Opens for animal storage

Noah

Slumber party

Elizabeth and Felicity love to spend the night at each other's houses. The girls help look after Felicity's baby sister, Polly. They even rock Polly to sleep in her cradle.

BEHIND THE SCENES

Author Kathleen Ernst went to great lengths to accurately describe Caroline's life on Lake Ontario 200 years ago. She is pictured here helping steer the *Friends Good Will*—a working reproduction of a sloop, just like a sailboat that Caroline would have known.

Main sail

Oars for rowing

SPENCER JACKET
When chilly lake winds pick up, Caroline wears her cropped Spencer jacket to stay warm as she sails.

Set sail

Caroline enjoys sailing on Lake Ontario. From her skiff, Caroline watches big ships glide across the harbor. She imagines being on board one of the ships herself one day—as the captain!

SAILING SKIFF
Caroline's father runs a shipyard on the shores of Lake Ontario. He builds a small boat called a skiff and names it "Miss Caroline" after his daughter.

Lake skating

Even though she can't sail the open waters during the winter, Caroline still flies across the frozen lake. With blades strapped to her boots, Caroline's ordinary shoes become ice skates.

Josefina
Montoya™ *1824*

Pendant from Mexico City

Golden hoop earrings

After gaining independence from Spanish rule, New Mexico welcomes *Americanos*, people from the United States, for the first time. Life on Josefina's family rancho is busy. While she dreams of becoming a healer, Josefina must also learn to be open to new ideas.

Josefina's pouch

Fringed *rebozo* (wrap)

Embroidered hankie

Accessories

A long, fringed *rebozo* covers Josefina's head from the sun when it's hot, and keeps her warm on cool evenings. Josefina proudly wears the pendant that her aunt brought back from Mexico City.

Blanket weaving

Josefina learns how to weave warm blankets using colored yarn and a loom.

Shuttle carries yarn from one side of the loom to the other

Loom

Weaving fork for tightening woven yarn

Moccasins

Black lace mantilla (thin veil)

Fancy comb

Josefina's doll, Niña

TREASURES

Josefina keeps her most precious items in her bedroom. Her doll, Niña, was made by her mamá.

Notebook from Josefina's aunt containing Mamá's special sayings

Quill and ink

Candle holder

Christmas dress

Josefina enjoys sewing and making clothes for herself. When her aunt gives Josefina some striped fabric, Josefina makes a dress to wear on *Noche Buena*, Christmas Eve—the most special night of the year on the rancho.

MEET
Josefina

NAME
María Josefina Montoya

BIRTH YEAR
1815

HOMETOWN
Near Santa Fe, New Mexico

BIGGEST DREAM
To be a healer

FAMILY
Father, Ana, Francisca, and Clara (sisters), Dolores and Magdalena (aunts)

Did you know?
In 1824, New Mexico was part of Mexico, not the United States. New Mexico didn't become a state until almost 100 years later, in January 1912.

Nightfall

When night falls on the rancho, Josefina is tucked up beneath a colorful blanket, and she has sweet dreams on her soft mattress, called a *colchon*. A cozy rug is the perfect spot to say good night to her pet goat, Sombrita.

SOMBRITA

Josefina's black-and-white goat is named Sombrita. This is Spanish for "little shadow," because the goat follows Josefina wherever she goes!

Feast of San José

Instead of celebrating her birthday, Josefina celebrates the feast day of *San José*, the saint she was named after. Helping Josefina look her best, her sisters bring out Mamá's embroidered shawl and black fan, treasures saved just for special occasions.

Mano and *metate* (grinding stones)

Mantón (shawl)

Mamá's fan

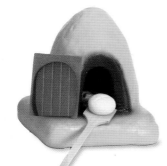

OUTDOOR COOKING
Josefina and her family use an outdoor oven called a *horno* for baking.

Traditional New Mexican decoration

BEHIND THE SCENES

An esteemed advisory panel of historians and museum professionals contributed more than their professional insights and memories with the American Girl staff. So product designers could perfect Josefina's hair, one advisor went so far as to clip a lock of his own hair to provide a sample.

Family fiesta

Whether it's a family dinner or special fiesta, Josefina enjoys the hustle and bustle of working in the *cocina*, or kitchen. Together, Josefina and her three sisters make traditional New Mexican foods, such as tortillas, using fresh ingredients gathered from their kitchen garden.

In the garden

Josefina and her family grow plants and flowers on their rancho. Josefina enjoys caring for the plants, just like Mamá used to. Sometimes, Josefina picks pretty flowers to bring inside.

Marie-Grace

Gardner™ *1853*

Marie-Grace is a quiet, shy girl growing up in the diverse community of New Orleans, Louisiana. When she makes friends with confident, outgoing Cécile Rey, Cécile encourages Marie-Grace to open up and have fun.

MEET
Marie-Grace

NAME
Marie-Grace Rousseau Gardner

BIRTH YEAR
1843

HOMETOWN
New Orleans, Louisiana

BIGGEST DREAM
To make a difference to others

FAMILY
Father,
Luc and Océane
(uncle and aunt)

ARGOS
Marie-Grace's uncle rescued this cute dog when he was a puppy. Marie-Grace named him Argos, and they've been inseparable ever since.

Mardi Gras

New Orleans is well known for its music, colorful homes, and Mardi Gras balls. This big celebration marks the 40 days of fasting before Easter. Marie-Grace and Cécile are excited to put on their costumes and masks, dance, eat sweets, and watch the fireworks.

Taffeta dress

Parlor Fun

Cécile enjoys spending her free time in the parlor. Her colorful pet parrot, Cochon, keeps Cécile company while she reads or plays games.

Cochon

Jenny Lind paper dolls

Special Desk

Cécile keeps all of her treasures, including her paper dolls, tucked away in the hidden compartment of her parlor desk.

Cécile
Rey™ *1853*

Knee-length stockings

Cécile Rey is born to be on stage! She loves parties and can't wait for the grand Children's Ball held for Mardi Gras. When she makes a new friend in Marie-Grace, Mardi Gras season turns out to be even more exciting than she expected.

Summer days

Summers in New Orleans can be very warm, but that doesn't stop Marie-Grace and Cécile from enjoying the outdoors. Picnics, outdoor games, special treats, and time with friends and family are still full of fun—even under the hot summer sun.

Bonnet

Winter ball

When the girls are invited to a winter ball, Marie-Grace worries that she has nothing to wear. Luckily, Cécile comes to the rescue with the perfect matching blue-and-pink outfits.

Lemon taffeta dress

PRETTY PARASOL
To help create some shade from the hot sun, Marie-Grace opens her cream-colored lacy parasol with a sculpted golden handle.

Wide-brimmed hat

Scrollwork detail

Three-tiered skirt

BEHIND THE SCENES

The book authors and project team from American Girl toured historic houses and museums in New Orleans to learn about the city's history, culture, and unique architecture, including courtyards like this one.

55

New school

At first, Kirsten finds it difficult to adjust to school in Minnesota. Between lessons, Kirsten's classmates play games outdoors. Always excited to try new things, Kirsten joins in the fun. She soon makes new friends and settles in.

Friendship quilt

Having made new friends in Minnesota, Kirsten feels more like an American. For her birthday Kirsten's friends give her a quilt. It's signed, "For Kirsten Larson on her 10th birthday."

Did you know?
Swedish immigrants owned just enough utensils for their own families. They could not bring much with them on their voyage. Guests carried their own utensils in spoon bags when they went to other immigrants' homes for parties.

Embroidery hoop with fabric

TRUNK
Kirsten's family brought this trunk all the way from Sweden. They keep their treasures in it.

Kirsten's cat, Missy, and her kitten

Red-checked sunbonnet

Amber-colored heart from Kirsten's grandmother

Kirsten
Larson™ *1854*

With a pioneering spirit, Kirsten and her family leave their home in Sweden to set sail for America. After many months of traveling, they finally arrive at their new home in the Minnesota Territory. Everything in the New World is strange, but friends and family help Kirsten find the true meaning of home.

Spoon bag embroidered with Kirsten's initials: "K.L."

Summer fun

Kirsten has to wear warm, heavy clothes all winter long. When summer arrives, Kirsten can't wait to pull on her light summer dress.

MEET
Addy

NAME
Addy Walker

BIRTH YEAR
1855

HOMETOWN
Philadelphia, Pennsylvania

BIGGEST DREAM
To help her family stay close

FAMILY
Momma, Poppa,
Sam (brother),
Esther (sister)

Birthday treat

Momma organizes a special treat for Addy's first birthday in freedom. Momma makes a special pinafore dress, and they celebrate with all of Addy's favorite treats.

Snood with ribbon trim

Ice cream freezer

Checked pinafore

New school

Addy's new life in Philadelphia brings friends and, for the first time, school. Her mother packs her a special lunch every day. Addy quickly catches up with the other children in her class, and she is so proud to win the school spelling bee.

Did you know?
Like many children born into slavery, Addy doesn't know her own birthday, so she chooses a day. She picks April 9, the day the Civil War ended in 1865 and all slaves were freed.

Spelling bee outfit made by Momma

School lunch pail

Bedside lamp

BEDTIME
Some nights, Addy reads *Mother Goose in Hieroglyphics*, when she is tucked in bed with Ida Bean—the rag doll Momma made for her.

Addy
Walker™ *1864*

Addy grows up in a time of great change, as the Civil War is just beginning. Her family plans a daring escape from slavery, but before they can get away, they are separated. Addy and Momma escape north to Philadelphia, where slavery is illegal, and begin a new life as free people. Believing her family will one day be together again gives Addy strength.

Great-grandmother's necklace from Africa

Patchwork bag

Sunday best

Momma makes all of Addy's dresses with love and care. Addy chooses to wear this pretty purple dress and hat to church on Sundays.

Addy's freedom

Addy and Momma never give up the dream of having their family together in freedom. When Addy's father finds them, Addy is overjoyed. They move into a boarding house, where for the first time, Addy has a bed to call her own. Later reunited with her brother and sister, Addy finally has her whole family back.

BEHIND THE SCENES

Before product designers at American Girl used computers, doll outfits were sketched by hand. An early version of Addy's Christmas dress is shown here with a fabric swatch attached.

Nine-square fabric quilt

Christmas dress

Addy receives this beautiful dress as a gift from Momma's employer. Addy wears the fancy new dress to church for Christmas and brings her new doll, Ida Bean—a gift from Momma—along, too.

FAMILY QUILT

Addy's colorful quilt shows the faces and places that represent her family. Addy lays the quilt on her very own bed with pride.

SLEEP TIGHT

Addy's comfortable mattress rests on ropes instead of springs. She tightens the ropes to keep her bed from sagging.

Warm nightgown

Samantha
Parkington™ *1904*

Samantha would rather be climbing trees than acting like the proper young lady girls are expected to be in the early 1900s. Always ready to make a new friend, Samantha is happy to lend a hand to someone in need, even if it means ruffling a few feathers.

Walk in the park
Samantha's hat shades her face from the sun while she's walking Jip, her cocker spaniel, in the park.

Helping hand
When Samantha befriends her next door neighbor, Nellie, Samantha learns that Nellie can't attend school because she works as a servant. Samantha thinks this is unfair, so she decides to help Nellie learn to read and write.

Double-breasted school dress

School desk

Book strap for carrying school supplies

SCHOOLWORK
Samantha shares her school composition and reading books with Nellie to help with her lessons.

Before bed

Samantha loves spending time in her bedroom. She can relax before bedtime with her teddy bear, music box, and her favorite book, *The Wizard of Oz*.

Heart-shaped locket from her family

Did you know?

Teddy bears, named for President Theodore "Teddy" Roosevelt, were a popular toy in Samantha's day. Samantha's bear wears a pink ribbon.

MEET
Samantha

NAME
Samantha Mary Parkington

BIRTH YEAR
1895

HOMETOWN
Mount Bedford, New York

BIGGEST DREAM
To help those in need

FAMILY
Grandmary (grandmother), Gardner and Cornelia (uncle and aunt)

Purse with golden clasp and chain

PURSE

Samantha's dresses don't have pockets so she carries small items, such as coins and a handkerchief, in her purse.

In the garden

Samantha enjoys spending sunny afternoons outside in her grandmother's beautiful garden. The pretty white gazebo is the perfect place to paint or just relax in the shade with refreshments.

BEHIND THE SCENES

Author Valerie Tripp grew up in Mt. Kisco, New York and she passed this house every day on her way to school. The Victorian home inspired the one she wrote about in Samantha's stories.

Ice cream parlor

As a special treat, Samantha visits Tyson's Ice Cream Parlor in New York City with her aunt and uncle. She can sit at the counter to enjoy a range of delightful sweets.

PRETTY LANTERNS
Colored lanterns light up the gazebo as night falls.

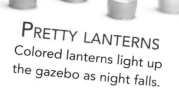

BUDDING ARTIST
Samantha sets up her easel in the garden and paints beautiful watercolor pictures.

Painting set

Serving cart

Pansy decoration
to match bag

Nellie
O'Malley™ *1906*

Coming from a poor family of Irish immigrants, Nellie has had to work from a young age. When she is hired to be a servant next door to Samantha Parkington's home, the two girls quickly become best friends. They live very different lives, but their friendship helps each other learn important lessons about themselves.

Drawstring
floral bag

Celtic cross
necklace

Irish penny

PRETTY ACCESSORIES
Nellie's hat shades her face when she's out in the summer sun. She always wears the Celtic cross necklace that once belonged to her mother.

Dotted
Swiss dress

Happy family
When Nellie's parents die from influenza, she takes a job as a house servant to earn money for herself and her younger sisters. When Samantha's uncle and aunt adopt them, Nellie can begin to enjoy her childhood. She is given this pretty dress as a gift for a spring party.

Pitcher and bowl for washing before bed

Embroidered flower trim

Lacy towel

Bedtime

Now Nellie isn't just Samantha's friend—they're family, too. The girls spend the nights whispering and giggling happily beneath the pretty lace-trimmed bedding.

Japanese-inspired kimono

MEET
Nellie

NAME
Nellie O'Malley

BIRTH YEAR
1895

HOMETOWN
New York, New York

BIGGEST DREAM
To keep her family together

FAMILY
Bridget and Jenny (sisters)

SLEIGH RIDE

As a winter treat, Nellie and Samantha go for a festive sleigh ride through Central Park. The sleigh bells jingle as they glide over the snow.

Did you know?

After the Great Famine in Ireland in 1845, millions of Irish families emigrated to the United States in search of a better life. Without money to travel farther, many settled in New York City, where the ships docked.

Shoulder cape

Holiday outfit

Nellie adores her winter coat. The black-and-white pleated plaid dress with a drop waist is perfect for celebrating Christmas. Nellie's red sash and matching hair bow add a festive touch.

Winter hat

Shoes with golden buckles

Rebecca

Rubin™ *1914*

In the 1910s, glamorous movie stars were more popular than ever. Rebecca loves watching movies and longs to be an actor, but her traditional Jewish family would rather she become a teacher. Rebecca looks for other ways to let her talents shine without disappointing her family or giving up on her dreams.

Grandmother's necklace from Russia

Pearly buttons

Sabbath candles

Sabbath dinner

For Rebecca and her family, it is important that they begin the Sabbath, a day of rest and worship, together. Every Friday night, Rebecca helps to prepare the Sabbath meal.

Rebecca

NAME
Rebecca Rubin

BIRTH YEAR
1905

HOMETOWN
New York, New York

BIGGEST DREAM
Shining bright for others

FAMILY
Mother, Father,
Sadie and Sophie (sisters),
Victor and Benny
(brothers), Max (cousin)

Summer day out

As a treat during summer vacation, Rebecca and her family spend the day at Coney Island in Brooklyn, New York. She keeps cool by the sea in her lavender dress and summer hat. Rebecca can't wait to try out all the rides at Steeplechase Park.

Carousel

Memory book

Ride ticket

Pretty postcards

SEASIDE SOUVENIRS

Rebecca's souvenirs from Coney Island mean she will never forget her fun day out.

Hanukkah party

Menorah

Rebecca is so excited to celebrate Hanukkah, the Jewish Festival of Lights, with her family. She is ready to light the candles in a special holder, which is called a menorah, and win shiny gelt in the dreidel game.

Gelt

Dreidel

A turquoise headdress, long gloves, and a pearly necklace are crowd-worthy finishing touches for any performance.

Movie star style curls

GOLDEN WINGS

Rebecca can transform from a young girl into a fairy princess with a pair of golden wings attached to her dress and overskirt.

BEHIND THE SCENES

Author Jaqueline Dembar Greene read early movie magazines and books for aspiring actors and actresses. The information she read, including tips on stage makeup, helped her make sure everything in Rebecca's story was picture perfect for her stage debut.

Golden ballet shoes

Movie costume

Showtime

Rebecca is so excited to visit a movie set with her actor cousin, Max. When the director needs a young girl for an upcoming scene, it's Rebecca's chance to take her fate into her own hands and step into the spotlight.

Costume chest

The movie studio has costumes to transform each actor into the perfect character. Rebecca is excited to see what's in the chest for her!

Butterfly Queen

Rebecca takes center stage in her school play, *The Butterfly Queen*. She impresses the audience in the leading role. A golden headband and beautiful wings make Rebecca feel like a star.

MEET Kit

NAME
Margaret "Kit" Mildred Kittredge

BIRTH YEAR
1923

HOMETOWN
Cincinnati, Ohio

BIGGEST DREAM
To turn hard times into good times

FAMILY
Mother, Father,
Charles (brother),
Hendrick and Millie
(uncle and aunt)

Scottie dog button

New dress

Kit is excited to go to the ballet at Christmas, but she's outgrown her old holiday dress and her family can't afford to buy a new one. Luckily, her best friend Ruthie gives her this beautiful dress to wear.

GRACE

Kit finds a basset hound that has been abandoned by her owner. Kit names the clumsy pooch Grace and is allowed to keep her.

Scooter

Clever Kit turns an old orange crate and a pair of roller skates into a scooter. There's even a seat for Grace. Together they roll around the neighborhood getting the scoop on local news.

BEHIND THE SCENES

Crafting Kit's character—from her hopes and dreams to her money-saving tricks—was very personal for author Valerie Tripp. Her mother was Kit's age in 1932. Valerie never wasted an opportunity to call her mom for inspiration and real-life perspective.

Birthday fun

With money so tight, Kit worries she can't have a 10th birthday party. That is until her aunt has an idea for a Penny Pincher Party—a simple picnic in the sun with her friends and family.

Cloche hat with red ribbon

Peter Pan collar

Kit
Kittredge™ *1934*

When her father loses his business during the Great Depression, times are difficult for Kit's family. Despite the challenges, Kit uses creativity and imagination to solve problems and help others. No matter what Kit is faced with, she can find the fun in any challenge.

Good news

Kit is tired of hearing bad news about the Depression, so she creates her own newspaper called the *Hard Times News*. She reports on the events of her house and neighborhood.

Flip-top notebook

Accordion-style camera

ACE REPORTER

Kit travels around her neighborhood looking for news. She always has her reporter's notebook and camera ready to catch a story.

Camera film

Kit's photographs

Tree house

Kit dreams of a backyard tree house, but supplies are scarce. When her dad builds one from old scraps, she's grateful, but it's not exactly what she had in mind. Instead of ditching her dream, Kit puts her creativity to work adding personal touches to make it a one-of-a-kind play spot.

TREE HOUSE STYLE
Kit decorates the tree house using items from around the house, such as photos, jars, and colorful beads.

Sturdy oak tree

Homemade crate scooter

Play day

Kit wears this floral dress when she plays outside in the summer. With little money for new clothes, Kit's mother makes the dress out of chicken-feed sacks.

Did you know?
During the Great Depression of the 1930s, around 13 million Americans were unemployed. Families struggled to get by, often making their own clothes, using scraps for building, and growing food in their backyards.

ORANGES
CALIFORNIA
Kit
Grace

Tree House Club sign

TREE HOUSE CLUB MEMBERS ONLY!

Stained-glass window

GIRLS' DAY
Kit and her best friend, Ruthie, get ready in the tree house for a special outing with their mothers to downtown Cincinnati.

Rope and bucket "elevator"

GOING UP
When Kit's dog, Grace, wants in on the Tree House Club fun, she sits in the bucket to be pulled up.

Ruthie
Smithens™ *1932*

The Great Depression means that many people are out of work and can barely afford to buy food. Ruthie's family is lucky because her dad has a good job. Still, that doesn't stop her from wanting to help others. Ruthie also loves to make her best friend, Kit, smile.

Did you know?
Many families took in boarders during the Great Depression. Renting rooms to paying guests provided much-needed income and allowed families to remain living in their homes.

Crocheted cloche hat

Talented team

Ruthie loves to work with Kit on her newspaper, the *Hard Times News*. Ruthie prefers to tell the stories and leave the typing to Kit.

Mary Jane shoes

Great friend

Ruthie wants to help when Kit's family takes in boarders. The extra money makes the family's life easier but means more work, too. Ruthie happily helps out with the extra laundry.

MEET
Ruthie

NAME
Ruthie Smithens

BIRTH YEAR
1923

HOMETOWN
Cincinnati, Ohio

BIGGEST DREAM
To help others during tough times

FAMILY
Mom and Dad

PLAY TIME

Ruthie enjoys playing with Kit outside. In this outfit, she is ready to share summertime adventures, and a smile, with her friend.

Belted tan knickers

Knee socks

Sleepover fun

Ruthie thinks her quiet house is so boring! She loves to stay over at Kit's so she can hear about what it's like to live with boarders. Ruthie thinks Kit's life is so much more exciting than her own.

Molly McIntire™ 1944

Locket with a picture of her father

Life during World War II is full of change. Molly's father is away caring for wounded soldiers, her mother is very busy helping the Red Cross gather supplies for the war effort, and a girl from England named Emily is staying with the McIntires. Luckily, Molly is full of big ideas to get them through the tough times.

Did you know?

Many people wanted to help the war effort. They planted Victory Gardens so that food from farms could go to soldiers. Some foods, such as sugar, were in short supply and were used only for special occasions.

Tea party

Molly and her friend Emily host a party for Molly's birthday. They wear pretty party pinafores and shiny red-and-gold birthday crowns.

Christmas box

Although her father can't be with them on Christmas Day, Molly and her family receive a surprise package from him. It is filled with beautiful gifts for the family. Molly gets the nurse doll of her dreams.

Evergreen Christmas dress

Nurse doll

Christmas snow globe

In the classroom

Molly tries to do her best in everything, and schoolwork is no exception. She finds math very hard. Molly does not give up easily and has a great idea—she uses flash cards to get better at multiplication.

Name tag

English notebook

Math flash cards

SCHOOL BAG

Molly carries her schoolwork in a messenger bag. Her name is written on the front so she never loses it.

Tent tidiness

The Camp Gowonagin tent motto is "Tidy and True." Molly makes sure to always keep her tent clean and her belongings in order. On camp cleaning day, she rolls open the sides for easy sweeping of the plank floors.

CAMP TENT
Tent No. 6 is Molly's home away from home while she spends two weeks of summer fun at Camp Gowonagin.

Camp Gowonagin logo

Camp logo cap

Roll-up window flaps

Camp equipment bag

CAMP GOWONAGIN

SLEEPING BAG
Molly brings her father's sleeping bag to keep her cozy on cool nights.

Plaid flannel lining

Summer camp

With her father away and her mother working, Molly spends two weeks of her summer vacation at Camp Gowonagin with her friends. Molly loves camp from the moment she arrives. She learns many new skills, such as first aid. Molly even finds the strength to overcome her fear of swimming underwater.

Tie-back tent doors

BEHIND THE SCENES

When Pleasant T. Rowland and Valerie Tripp were developing the original American Girl characters, Kirsten, Samantha, and Molly, Valerie insisted that one of the characters needed to wear glasses. She chose Molly because she liked the way the glasses looked with Molly's braids.

TENT NO. 6

Pup-sized first aid kit

K-9

FIRST AID

PUP TENT
Molly enjoys sleeping in her tent so much that she makes a mini one for her dog, Bennett!

Bennett's PUP TENT

Beach fun

After camp is over, Molly and her friend Emily find there's still plenty of summer fun to be had. They put on their swimsuits and grab a beach ball for a fun day at the lake.

83

Emily
Bennett™ *1944*

Cherry blossom decorations

Emily lives in London during World War II, until the city is bombed and it is no longer safe. She's sent to America to live with her aunt, but Emily has to stay with the McIntire family while Aunt Primrose recovers from pneumonia. Emily must learn to be brave in her new home.

Ration book

Grandfather's dog tags from World War I

Dress from Aunt Primrose

Treasures

When Emily first arrives at Molly's house, she is homesick. Emily treasures her keepsakes, including photos of the two British princesses, her grandfather's dog tags, a ration book with a note from her mother, and a British coin.

New friends

Emily tries to be brave, but she really wants to go home. With a little kindness and understanding from Molly, Emily starts to feel at home. The two become good friends.

Bennett

Yank

TERRIER PUPS

Molly and Emily are each given a Jack Russell terrier puppy. Emily names hers Yank, the nickname for Americans in England. Molly names hers Bennett, after Emily.

Did you know?
Many children living in London were evacuated from the city during World War II to escape the bombing. Some children were sent overseas or to the countryside where it was safer. They returned to their families after the war.

MEET
Emily

NAME
Emily Bennett

BIRTH YEAR
1933

HOMETOWN
London, England

BIGGEST DREAM
To be with her family again

FAMILY
Mother, Father, Grandy and Grandmum (grandfather and grandmother), Primrose (aunt)

Cold winter

The cold Illinois winter is a shock to Emily—it rarely snows in London. Emily and Molly have fun ice skating on the frozen lake, sledding, and making snow angels. Her snowsuit, snow boots, and mittens keep Emily warm.

At home

When Maryellen is at home relaxing, she loves to snuggle up in front of the TV on the family's sofa bed.

HAIRSTYLING

Before she goes to bed, Maryellen puts in her curlers. When she wakes up in the morning, she'll have perfect curls!

Cap keeps curlers in place

Curlers

SCOOTER

Maryellen's lovable dachshund dog, Scooter, follows Maryellen around wherever she goes.

TV antenna

ON TV

Maryellen and her family gather around the TV to watch their favorite shows. If there's nothing on, they can listen to music on the built-in record player.

Built-in record player

Shrug embroidered with an "M" for Maryellen

Maryellen
Larkin™ 1954

With modern technology, such as TV sets and new fashions, Maryellen is excited about the changes the 1950s bring. Comparing her life to TV shows means she has a head full of pie-in-the sky ideas! Maryellen stays true to herself and what she believes, and that means only the sky's the limit.

New dress

For her ninth birthday Maryellen gets a real surprise—a beautiful new green dress! She can't wait to wear something that isn't a hand-me-down from her sisters.

MEET
Maryellen

NAME
Maryellen Larkin

BIRTH YEAR
1945

HOMETOWN
Daytona Beach, Florida

BIGGEST DREAM
To inspire others to stand out from the crowd

FAMILY
Mom, Dad,
Joan, Beverly, Carolyn (sisters),
Tom and Mikey (brothers)

Frozen fun

Maryellen's holiday wish is to go ice-skating and it comes true! To keep warm, she wears an old stocking cap she found tucked away in her mom's closet.

Seaside Diner

After school, Maryellen loves to hang out at the Seaside Diner with her friends and sisters. At this hip spot she can sit in a booth, order a milkshake, and watch the cook slide orders through the pickup window.

BEHIND THE SCENES

To develop "TV shows" for Maryellen's Television, product designers used real samples of the Seaside Diner. Other toys were used to create music videos of Maryellen dancing with her dog, Scooter.

Handwriting

Maryellen practices writing on the chalkboard in class. She is learning to write in cursive, but it isn't easy to do because Maryellen is left-handed.

HOT DOG

A big family means hand-me-downs for Maryellen. So she's thrilled when her mom buys Maryellen her own poodle skirt.

Polka-dot kerchief

ROCK AND ROLL
Maryellen loves to play popular songs on the diner's colorful jukebox.

Pink poodle with stitched leash

Black-and-white saddle shoes

Church choir

Melody gets dressed up in her Sunday best for church. She adds her voice to the choir, standing up for what she believes is right.

Freedom march

Melody attends a freedom march in Detroit with her family to support the fight for equality.

Equal rights button

SIXTIES STYLE

Melody wears turquoise accessories to the freedom march, and a button to show she supports equal rights. Melody's cat-eye sunglasses make her feel like a star!

MEET
Melody

NAME
Melody Ellison

BIRTH YEAR
1954

HOMETOWN
Detroit, Michigan

BIGGEST DREAM
To use her voice to stand up for equality

FAMILY
Mom, Dad,
Yvonne and Lila (sisters),
Dwayne (brother)

Time for bed

Melody's baby-doll style PJs and pom-pom slippers are perfect for bedtime. She loves her orange-and-gold bedspread and plaid headboard doors.

Melody
Ellison™ 1964

Melody lifts up her voice to speak out for equal rights for African-Americans in her hometown of Detroit, Michigan, during the civil rights movement. Melody works together with people from many different backgrounds, and she learns that even the smallest voice can make a big difference.

Houndstooth minidress

Did you know?
Dr. Martin Luther King, Jr. was a leader of the civil rights movement in the 1950s and 1960s. He first gave his famous "I Have a Dream" speech in Detroit in 1963.

Best friends
Melody's pup, Bo, is a mixed terrier full of playful energy. He's named after Bill "Bojangles" Robinson, a famous African-American tap dancer and actor. Melody loves to take Bo for walks around her neighborhood.

Music maker

Whether it's singing or tapping on a tambourine, Melody loves to make music. She aspires to be just like her brother Dwayne, who wants to be a famous singer with one of Detroit's big record companies. When Dwayne gets the opportunity to sing for a record label, Melody gets to add her voice, too.

Make our Neighborhood Bloom!

Community spirit

Melody's family is part of their neighborhood block club, which works together to improve the local area. Sometimes, they get together to have block parties with delicious food, exciting games, and plenty of noisy fun.

STUDIO TIME
When Melody's brother, Dwayne, records a new song, he asks her to be his backup singer. Melody can't believe her luck!

SOUNDS GOOD
Music is very important to Melody and her family. Melody's grandmother is teaching her to play the piano, just like her brother.

BEHIND THE SCENES
Author Denise Lewis Patrick grew up in Louisiana. She tapped into her childhood experiences and family history in the South to breathe life into Melody's stories. Denise also worked closely with advisory panel members who grew up in Detroit and who were active in the civil rights movement.

SING ALONG
From church hymns to the latest hits, Melody is happiest when she's singing.

Tinted
sunglasses

Braided
headband

Julie
Albright™ *1974*

New fashion, music, and attitudes
in the 1970s offer changing times for
Julie. When her parents get divorced,
she has to move to a different
area of San Francisco with
her mom. Julie misses her
dad, but with her sunny
spirit and bright outlook
on life, she is determined to
make a fresh start.

Tie-dye
purse

Bell-bottom
pants

New room

Julie loves dreaming in her new bedroom.
Her favorite spot to unwind is in her stereo
egg chair. Julie sings along to favorite tunes
playing from the built-in speakers.

Car wash

Julie will always stand up for others—and that includes animals. So when her school decides to raise money to save two bald eagles, Julie grabs buckets, sponges, soap, and her friends for a charity car wash.

Did you know?
Clothing for women and girls in the 1970s was more casual and loose fitting than in previous decades. T-shirts, jeans, and peasant-style dresses were common items in a girl's everyday wardrobe.

Woven sun hat

Happy birthday

Julie has the perfect outfit to wear to her birthday celebration on the beach. She wears a free-flowing peasant dress with a flower-print border and wide-brimmed hat to block the California sun.

NUTMEG
Julie loves her chocolate-colored, lop-eared bunny, Nutmeg. Julie spoils him with plenty of special treats.

Picnic basket

Game day

Julie's new school won't let her play on the basketball team—it's for boys only—but Julie won't take no for an answer. She practices hard and starts a petition to make her hoop dreams come true. When she finally puts on her uniform, the bleachers fill with fans to cheer her on.

Jaguars team jersey

Sports bag

Striped sneakers

Disco time

After the big game, the sports hall is transformed for a school dance. In the light of a mirrored spinning disco ball, Julie shows off her groovy moves in a flower-print dress and woven belt.

Basketball scoreboard

Cheer banner

School spirit pennant

SCHOOL LUNCH
Julie's lunch travels in far-out style in a flower-power lunch box and matching insulated bottle.

After-school snack

After school, Ivy loves hanging out at her best friend Julie's house—it's very different from her family home. The girls relax with a tasty snack and discuss their day at school.

Calico-print dress

Swivel chair

Chinese New Year

Ivy's family always has a big party to celebrate Chinese New Year. Ivy's shimmering red silk dress is a special gift for the New Year celebrations.

Red paisley bandanna

Did you know?
At Chinese New Year, families get together to celebrate. Red is the color for good luck in China. Houses are decorated in red paper cuttings symbolizing happiness, good fortune, and long life.

MEET
Ivy

NAME
Ivy Ling

BIRTH YEAR
1966

HOMETOWN
San Francisco, California

BIGGEST DREAM
To make her family proud

FAMILY
Mom, Dad, Andrew (brother), Missy (sister), Gung Gung and Po Po (grandfather and grandmother)

Fashion sense

Ivy likes to get creative and make her own clothes. She customized this romper by adding a fashionable rainbow belt and red pointed collar.

Funky orange flip-flops

98

Ivy Ling™ 1976

Ivy Ling wants her family to be proud of her and their Chinese heritage is very important to her. But when a big gymnastics tournament falls on the same day as her family reunion, Ivy has to learn how to balance her present with her past.

Chandelier earrings

Purse made from old jeans

Bike ride

On the weekend Ivy spends time with her best friend, Julie. They take turns riding Julie's banana seat bike in the park.

Super sets

Since the launch of the historical dolls in 1986, thousands of wonderfully detailed accessories have brought the dolls' stories—and America's rich history—to life.

Smallest

RELEASE DATE: 2009

REBECCA'S RABBIT PIN
The accessory most dear to Rebecca is a rabbit pin—a special gift from her grandmother. At ¾ inches wide, it's also one of the smallest accessories produced.

Tiled roof

TREE HOUSE CLUB MEMBERS ONLY!

Lifelike leaves

Biggest

KIT'S TREE HOUSE
Kit's Tree House was not only a big hit with Kit fans—it was also big in size! At 36 inches wide, 37 inches tall, and 23 inches deep, this dream playhouse was the perfect place for Kit to spend time with her friends.

Grace's bucket

RELEASE DATE: 2008

Most items

MOLLY'S CURL KIT

It takes a lot of work—and many accessories—for a perfectly styled look. With 30 pieces, Molly's curl kit was the historical set with the most items.

Pretend hair dryer

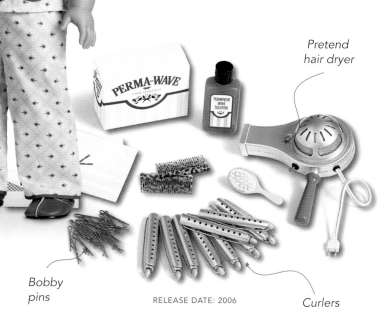

Bobby pins

RELEASE DATE: 2006

Curlers

KIRSTEN'S CATS

The mother cat, and her tiny kitten, in Kirsten's set were the first pets released along with Molly's dog.

RELEASE DATE: 1988
(PICTURED: 2000)

MOLLY'S DOG

Bennett, Molly's playful pup, was released at the same time as Kirsten's cats, making him the first dog in the American Girl collections.

RELEASE DATE: 1988
(PICTURED: 2000)

Biggest collection

The Wizard of Oz book

Jip

RELEASE DATE: 2014

SAMANTHA

Samantha first launched in 1986. In 2014 she was re-released with a whole new collection. Of all the BeForever™ dolls, Samantha has had the most outfits, accessories, and pieces of furniture.

Garden furniture

RELEASE DATE: 2014

Ice cream parlor

RELEASE DATE: 2014

RELEASE DATE: 1988

Lindsey Bergman™ 2001   *Kailey Hopkins™ 2003*   *Marisol Luna™ 2005*   *Jess McConnell™ 2006*

Gwen Thompson™ 2009   *Lanie Holland™ 2010*   *Kanani Akina™ 2011*   *McKenna Brooks™ 2012*

Nicki Fleming™ 2007

Mia St. Clair™ 2008

Chrissa Maxwell™ 2009

Sonali Matthews™ 2009

Girl of the Year™

Saige Copeland™ 2013

Isabelle Palmer™ 2014

Grace Thomas™ 2015

Lea Clark™ 2016

Each year, a new Girl of the Year is released who shares the interests and hobbies of today's girls. The Girl of the Year characters inspire girls to dream big and make a difference—whether it's standing up to bullying with Chrissa or diving into new adventures with Lea.

More stories

Marisol was released with just one book. By 2014, Girl of the Year, Isabelle, had three stories.

Marisol Luna™, 2005

Changes over time

The first two dolls, Lindsey and Kailey, were introduced two years apart as the first contemporary characters. Beginning with Marisol in 2005, a new character is released each year. With Marisol, American Girl launched the Girl of the Year line.

Different interests

Just as real girls have lots of interests, the Girls of the Year do, too. Some love outdoor adventures such as boogie boarding or horseback riding, others practice gymnastics or dance. Whatever their interests, the dolls encourage girls to try something new and express themselves.

Lea's rainforest house

Expanding collections

As the Girl of the Year line grew in popularity, their collections grew, too. In 2001, Lindsey came with a single outfit, a scooter, and a laptop. Fifteen years later, Lea's collection includes five additional outfits, a kayak, hiking gear, beach accessories, a fruit stand, and a rainforest house.

Lea's kayak

Left: Lea; Right: Lanie

Scooting around

Lindsey's scooter gets her to school and all around town. She wears gloves to help grip the handles, and she never forgets her butterfly helmet.

Did you know?

Kick scooters—powered by pushing off the ground—have been around for over a hundred years. The earliest ones were made by attaching roller skate wheels to a wooden plank and adding a handlebar.

Lindsey

NAME
Lindsey Bergman

BIRTH YEAR
1991

HOMETOWN
Chicago, Illinois

BIGGEST DREAM
To make the world a better place

FAMILY
Mom, Dad,
Ethan (brother),
Bernie (uncle)

Messenger bag

Laptop

LAPTOP

Lindsey's computer is also great for helping with her schoolwork.

THURSDAY
10-18-2001
A 11-30 47

High tech

Whatever plan Lindsey comes up with, she notes it on her laptop. She carries it in her messenger-style computer bag, along with a pencil and notebook.

Beaded bobby pin

Lindsey
Bergman™ *2001*

Lindsey has big ideas and a passion for helping others. Her good intentions don't always go according to plan, but Lindsey's heart is always in the right place. Sometimes Lindsey gets too involved in other people's lives. However, she soon learns the difference between meddling and truly helping.

BEHIND THE SCENES

Lindsey Bergman scooted off the catalogue page and into the hearts of American girls looking for stories about girls growing up today. Little did the team that developed Lindsey know just how popular the future Girl of the Year™ line would come to be.

Drawstring hem

Girl on the go

Lindsey doesn't like to sit still for long, and climbing trees and riding scooters require comfy clothes. Her "love dogs" tee, khaki skirt, hooded zip-up sweater, and striped tights are perfect for a girl on the move.

Buckled ankle boots

Kailey
Hopkins™ 2003

Athletic Kailey lives for the beach and exploring the rocky tide pools. When she hears a resort will be built at her favorite beach spot, she fears it will harm the tide pools and the creatures living in them. Kailey has to find the courage to stand up for the coastline she loves.

Double braids

Beaded necklace

Embroidered flowers

Under the sea

Kailey loves everything to do with the beach! Snorkeling is one of her favorite hobbies—she loves floating on her front and looking down through her goggles at the crystal-clear world below.

Snorkel goggles

Underwater camera

Flippers

Crocheted sandals

MEET
Kailey

NAME
Kailey Hopkins

BIRTH YEAR
1993

HOME
Southern California

BIGGEST DREAM
To save the tide pools

FAMILY
Mom and Dad

Sandy
Kailey's dog is named after one of Kailey's favorite things: The sandy beach! Sandy wears a purple bandanna around his neck. He loves being at he beach as much as Kailey.

Starfish embroidered bag

Beaded anklet

Purple bandanna

Suited up
Kailey puts on her wet suit and water socks when she explores the tide pools at the beach. They help her stay warm in the chilly water and protect her feet.

Did you know?
Tide pools form in the holes and crevices of rocks when the tide goes out. Each pool is home to lots of creatures, including hermit crabs, sea urchins, and bat stars—a type of starfish.

Water socks

Storage bag

Board wax

Riding waves
Kailey goes boogie boarding as often as she can. She races into the water and lies on the board to ride an incoming wave. Kailey applies wax to her board to keep it from getting too slippery.

109

Marisol
Luna™ *2005*

Marisol was born to dance! There's nothing she enjoys more than her dance classes. When Marisol moves to a neighborhood without a dance studio, she's devastated. Luckily, she doesn't give up easily. Marisol convinces a local dancer to teach dance lessons in her new hometown.

Rascal

Crocheted scarf

Adhesive bandages

Cargo pants

Carry all

Marisol's duffel holds all of her essentials for dance class, including a water bottle, cell phone, and first aid supplies. It's also the perfect place to keep her dance academy ID tag. Sometimes, Marisol's cat, Rascal, curls up in the bag, too!

Practice makes perfect

Marisol is new to ballet, and she finds the strict classes difficult. But she learns that ballet is the basis for all types of serious dance, so Marisol works hard. She heads to classes in a pretty pink practice outfit.

MEET
Marisol

NAME
Marisol Luna

BIRTH YEAR
1995

HOMETOWN
Chicago, Illinois

BIGGEST DREAM
To be a real dancer on stage

FAMILY
Mom and Dad

Did you know?
Marisol also dances ballet folklórico with a Mexican folk dance troupe. Ballet folklórico has some of the same movements as ballet, but it is not as strict. Each Mexican region has its own traditional dances.

AMERICAN GIRL THEATER

PERFORMANCE TRUNK
Marisol keeps all of her dance outfits, accessories, and certificates in her trunk.

All that jazz

In her jazz outfit, Marisol is ready to hit the stage! The shimmery top and purple pants make her feel like a star—especially when she adds a feather boa.

Big dreams

Marisol's dream is to become a professional dancer. Whether she's twirling through a leaf pile or tap-dancing across her bedroom floor, Marisol imagines that she's peforming for a crowd. She knows that her dream will take hard work, but Marisol is determined to make it come true.

Tap time

Marisol shines in her tap outfit, with a fringe skirt, fishnet tights, a glittery top hat, and a cane. After she puts on her bow tie, Marisol is ready to perform.

Ribbon
choker

TWINKLING TIARA
A sparkly tiara catches the light and makes Marisol shine more brightly when she takes the stage.

Rhinestone-
studded tutu

PRETTY SLIPPERS
Purple ballet slippers match Marisol's beautiful leotard, tutu, and lavender tights.

Jess
McConnell™ 2006

Jess is excited to go to Belize in Central America with her parents. She has never been on a trip outside of the United States before, and Jess is nervous about traveling without her older brother and sister for the first time. But she is ready to explore a new place and have a real adventure.

Bag with maps and airplane tickets

Butterfly-shaped camera

Guidebook

Packed and ready

Jess's canvas shoulder bag holds everything she needs for an adventure in Belize: Her passport, plane tickets, maps, guidebook, and camera. A water bottle is a must in the hot jungle!

Sandal with braided strap

MEET
Jess

NAME
Jess Akiko McConnell

BIRTH YEAR
1996

HOMETOWN
Houghton, Michigan

BIGGEST DREAM
To explore the world

FAMILY
Mom, Dad,
Heather (sister),
Jason (brother),
Grandma Emi

Adventure time

Jess has lots of fun in Belize. She tries adventurous new activities—even kayaking down a river. Trying different things teaches Jess that she is brave and confident.

TOSHI

Jess befriends a spider monkey named Fuzz. Her stuffed monkey, Toshi, looks just like the real spider monkey.

BEHIND THE SCENES

Traveling and experiencing the adventures she writes about is a critical part of author Mary Casanova's creative process. Just like Jess, Mary explored Belize.

In the swing

Jess's vacation home in Belize is different from her house in Michigan. Jess loves settling into the tree swing, and listening to the sounds of the jungle.

115

Exploring

While Jess's parents are on an archeological dig, she learns about the ancient Mayan peoples and their way of life. When she's not helping Mom and Dad, Jess is excited to explore her new surroundings and have plenty of fun along the way.

Did you know?
The ancient Mayan civilization existed a very long time ago. They lived in South America for 2,000 years, and made great scientific discoveries. Our modern calendar is based on theirs.

Scooter

Jungle explorer

With the help of her trusty guidebook and map, Jess and Toshi are ready to explore the jungle. Jess even hikes to the edge of a cenote—an ancient Mayan water source.

SCOOTER
Jess discovers she can explore even further on a motor scooter. She stores supplies, such as sunscreen, in the basket.

Jess uses her butterfly-shaped camera to take pictures of her time in Belize. She can't wait to share her photographs with everyone back home.

BELIZE

PASSPORT

Two-in-one kayaking outfit

★American Girl

Nicki

NAME
Nicki Fleming

BIRTH YEAR
1997

HOME
Near Denver, Colorado

BIGGEST DREAM
To help others

FAMILY
Mom, Dad,
Adam (brother),
Rebecca and Cristine
(sisters)

Long walks

Nicki takes Sprocket on long walks to her favorite meadow. There, Nicki and Sprocket sit by the stream. The sound of the gently flowing water is so relaxing!

Ski helmet

Hit the slopes

Nicki looks forward to ski season. The mountains around her ranch are perfect for skiing. Nicki wears warm layers and waterproof ski pants.

Ski pass

Clips for ski boots

Marker flags for races

SPECIAL SKIS

For her 10th birthday, Nicki's parents buy her a pair of colorful downhill skis.

Nicki
Fleming™ 2007

Nicki loves animals and helping others. When she gets the chance to train Sprocket the puppy as a service dog, she volunteers right away! It's a big job, but Nicki is happy to do it. She wants to help make other people's lives easier.

Did you know?
It takes a long time to train a service dog. Volunteers raise the puppies for about a year. Then, the dogs are specially trained for six to nine months before they are ready to help someone in need.

Out and about

Nicki dresses in cute clothes with a western flair. Sprocket wears a service-dog vest. The pocket holds a training log.

Western boots

Riding

Jackson, a beautiful brown horse, is another of Nicki's animal friends. Feeding him, grooming him, and cleaning out Jackson's stable takes a lot of time, but Nicki doesn't mind. Riding Jackson through the mountain meadows makes all of the hard work worthwhile.

Giddyup!

Nicki loves to ride Jackson. Before she can ride high in the saddle, Nicki must put on her riding gear, including long pants and her special riding boots.

BEHIND THE SCENES

Product designers jumped at the opportunity to develop a horse for Nicki. The horse's brand new mold suggested a more active pose, which had never been available from American Girl before.

Western-style saddle

CARE CASE
A blue tack box holds everything Nicki needs to take care of her horse, including Jackson's saddle and grooming supplies.

Duffel bag

Riding blanket

Chaps with
embroidered
flowers

GROOMING
Brushing Jackson's coat is
one of Nicki's favorite
chores. Jackson always
gets a treat afterward.

Mia
St. Clair™ 2008

Mia has spent years on the ice playing hockey with her three older brothers. But all Mia really wants to do is figure skate. It takes a lot of practice, but Mia proves that if she believes in herself and works hard, she can achieve her dreams of figure skating.

Practice clothes

Cozy pants, a fleece scarf, and mittens make the perfect practice outfit. A headband keeps Mia's hair out of her face while she practices routines.

Glitter snowflake

Thumbholes

High-top sneakers

Did you know?
Figure skating is the oldest sport in the Winter Olympic Games. Olympic figure skaters first took the ice in 1908. The sport has remained a part of the Games ever since.

Mia

NAME
Mia St.Clair

BIRTH YEAR
1998

HOME
Upstate New York

BIGGEST DREAM
To be a figure skater

FAMILY
Mom, Dad,
Perry, Skip, and Rick
(brothers)

Geared up

Mia needs her gear at lessons.
Her bag holds a music player,
headphones, and skate guards.
They protect the blades of her
skates when Mia is off the ice.

Music player

Music

Mia plays music while she practices
her skating routines. Her music player
has an armband so she can listen to
her favorite songs as she skates.

Built-in
closet

♥ Skating

Figure-skating
trophy

Cozy corner

After practice, Mia relaxes
in her bedroom. Surrounded
by posters and prizes, Mia
daydreams about skating.

Fold-out
bed

HOCKEY JERSEY
When she's playing ice hockey on the pond with her brothers, Mia wears a hockey shirt just like theirs.

SKATES
Mia wears her purple skates for figure-skating practice. She puts on a different pair when she plays ice hockey.

Ice hockey stick

Born to skate

Mia spends long hours at the rink practicing for her winter show performance. She also plays hockey with her big brothers just for fun. Mia picks up ice-skating tips from her brothers, and they encourage Mia to work hard. Whether she's playing hockey or figure skating, Mia loves being on the ice!

HAIR CARE

It's important for Mia to keep her hair pulled back neatly while she's figure skating. She stores handy accessories in this case.

BEHIND THE SCENES

Award-winning author Laurence Yep has loved figure skating since he was a kid. Laurence spoke with young skaters, watched plenty of competitions, and worked with a figure-skating coach to make sure Mia's stories were not only engaging and fun, but also accurate.

Sparkling star

At the winter show, Mia dazzles the crowd in her shimmery outfit. The audience loves watching Mia's super spins and jumps.

Chrissa
Maxwell™ 2009

When Chrissa's family moves from Iowa to her new home in Minnesota, she's nervous about starting at a new school and making friends. At first she gets picked on for being the new girl, but Chrissa learns to speak up for herself. She inspires her classmates to stand strong together against bullying.

Floral wrap dress

BEHIND THE SCENES

American Girl receives thousands of letters from girls saying how hard it can be to stand up to bullies. Chrissa's story shows how one girl can learn to handle difficult relationships.

New friends

Chrissa learns that being herself is the best way to make true friends. Before long, she has two new best friends: Sonali and Gwen.

Diving in

Chrissa loves being a part of the school swim club. When she finds out that some members of the swim team are being bullied, Chrissa stands up against the mean girls.

INSTANT MESSAGES

Chrissa loves making her friends smile. Homemade crafts and cards are always sure to cheer them up.

Goggles

Swim cap

SWIM GEAR

The swim club's colors are green and blue. Chrissa really makes a splash in her stylish swim gear.

Kickboard

Towel

Swimsuit

Celebrate new friends

MEET

Chrissa

NAME
Chrissa Maxwell

BIRTH YEAR
1999

HOMETOWN
Edgewater, Minnesota

BIGGEST DREAM
To stand strong against bullies

FAMILY
Mom, Dad,
Tyler (brother),
Nana (grandmother)

Winter chill

On cold winter days, Chrissa has fun playing in the snow. She wears cozy snow pants, a warm sweater, and a toasty hat and mittens. Chrissa is ready to explore her new hometown wearing a pair of sturdy snowshoes.

White turtleneck

Snow tube

SNOW FUN

Chrissa loves zipping down Minnesota's snowy hills in her inflatable snow tube. She holds onto the handles as she whooshes down slippery slopes.

127

SEWING MACHINE
Chrissa's sewing machine was a special gift from her nana.

LLAMA YARN
Chrissa's nana spins llama wool into yarn. Then she dyes the yarn with different colors. Chrissa and Nana knit with it.

Craft table

Chrissa's crafts

Chrissa loves working at the craft table in Nana's sunroom. The bright, airy space inspires her creativity and lets her ideas flow. She decorates throw pillows for her bed with shiny ribbons, knits cozy scarves, and makes special crafts with her grandmother.

Did you know?
To be considered miniature, llamas must be no more than 38 inches tall at shoulder height by the age of three. Standard-sized llamas can be much taller. They can reach up to six feet in height as adults.

Starburst

Chrissa's nana has three miniature llamas. The baby is Chrissa's pet, Starburst. Nana spins the llamas' wool into yarn. Then, Chrissa makes special things, such as a blanket for Starburst. It even has a pocket.

Sonali
Matthews™ *2009*

Cable-knit tunic

Sonali learns a lot about friendship when she leaves behind a group of mean girls and befriends Chrissa— the new girl at school. They both like to swim and picnic at the lake, especially with their friend Gwen.

MEET
Sonali

NAME
Sonali Matthews

BIRTH YEAR
1999

HOMETOWN
Edgewater, Minnesota

BIGGEST DREAM
To find true friends

FAMILY
Mom, Dad, two older sisters

Ballet flats

Summer celebration

Chrissa, Gwen, and Sonali celebrate their new friendship with a picnic by the lake. They enjoy a tasty meal together in the sunshine.

DECORATIONS
The friends decorate their picnic table with lanterns, and pretty cups and napkins.

Side by side

Gwen's new friend Chrissa helps Gwen find her voice. Both girls learn that they're stronger together—especially when it comes to making a stand against bullying.

MEET

Gwen

NAME
Gwen Thompson

BIRTH YEAR
1999

HOMETOWN
Edgewater, Minnesota

BIGGEST DREAM
To stand up to bullying

FAMILY
Mom

Gwen

Thompson™ 2009

Shy Gwen is being bullied at school, until Chrissa moves to town and becomes her friend. The new friends work together to make their school a friendlier place to be.

Flip-flops

Lanie
Holland™ 2010

Lanie dreams of being a scientist and protecting the environment. She wishes she could travel and explore the world. When Lanie learns more about her local environment, she realizes that she need only travel as far as her backyard to have an adventure.

ANIMAL LOVER
Lanie loves animals. She often takes her stuffed orangutan, Fio, with her to look for wildlife in the local area.

Nature journal

Picture this

The hammock in Lanie's backyard is a great place to observe nature. Monarch butterflies visit her beautiful wildflower garden. Lanie likes to sketch the pretty insects in her nature journal, and takes notes, too.

Letter from Aunt Hannah

LAPTOP
Lanie uses her laptop to look at all of the exciting places her aunt Hannah travels to.

BACKYARD ANIMALS
Lanie likes to keep an eye out for wildlife in her backyard. Sometimes, she's lucky enough to see red foxes.

Lanie

NAME
Lanie Holland

BIRTH YEAR
2000

HOMETOWN
Boston, Massachusetts

BIGGEST DREAM
To protect the Earth

FAMILY
Mom, Dad, Angela
and Emily (sisters),
Hannah (aunt)

Outdoor explorer

A striped cotton dress and canvas slip-ons are just right for exploring Lanie's big backyard. In her green messenger bag, Lanie keeps postcards from Aunt Hannah to inspire her. The bag also holds Lanie's nature journal and her laptop.

*Embroidered
dragonfly
patch*

*Heart charm
bracelet*

LULU

Lanie's pet rabbit, Lulu, hops beside her on a leash. Lulu even joins Lanie for nature walks.

NATURE HIKE

Lanie enjoys hiking and looking for birds. A colorful scarf keeps her warm on chilly spring days.

Did you know?
The first camper was made in 1910. It included a fold-down sink, a toilet, and a backseat, which could also be folded down to become a bed.

Postcards from around the world

HIDDEN BED
The bulletin board folds down into a bed when it's time to sleep.

Shower

RACCOONS
While she is camping, Lanie learns that she has to lock up the garbage to keep the hungry raccoons away!

Small refrigerator

please recycle

Summer fun

When Lanie's aunt, Hannah, visits for the summer, she teaches Lanie all about the local environment. Lanie loves learning about wildlife, nature, and how to care for her surroundings. Most of all, Lanie enjoys spending time with her amazing aunt, who loves being outdoors as much as she does.

EQUIPMENT
The camper holds lots of useful camping equipment—a sleeping bag, cooking supplies, and even a recycling bin!

Mirror

A home on wheels

Lanie loves Aunt Hannah's movable home! The camper has everything her aunt needs to live and work comfortably. She's always ready to drive off on her next adventure.

Kanani

Akina™ 2011

Kanani loves showing others the wonders of Hawai'i and spreading the joy, or "aloha spirit," of her home. Whether she is rescuing animals, strumming the ukulele, or helping her parents at their shop or stand, Kanani is always making others happy.

Hibiscus flower clip

Traditional Hawaiian necklace

Furry friend

Kanani enjoys spending time with her pet dog, Barksee. She rescued her lovable pup from the local dog pound.

MONK SEAL

The local newspaper writes a story about Kanani when she rescues a monk seal from a net.

DAILY BREEZE
Girls Rescue Monk Seal Pup

Kanani's local paper

MEET
Kanani

NAME
Kanani Akina

BIRTH YEAR
2001

HOMETOWN
Kauai, Hawai'i

BIGGEST DREAM
To spread the aloha spirit

FAMILY
Mom and Dad

Shave ice stand

Helping out at her family's shave ice stand is one of Kanani's favorite things to do. The money they make goes toward protecting endangered monk seals.

Menu

Poster

Postcard

Did you know?
Unlike a snow cone, which is crushed ice, the shave ice Kanani and her family make is very fine, like powdery snow. It is flavored with delicious, tropical syrups, such as passion fruit and mango.

BEACH TREATS
In addition to delicious treats, Kanani dishes out the aloha spirit with postcards and information on saving the monk seals.

Aloha spirit

Kanani discovers that she has a knack for brightening people's days and sharing her positive attitude with others. A day out at the beach with her friends and neighbors cheers everyone up. When she plays the ukulele, performs her hula dancing, and shares sweets from her parents' shop, Kanani spreads the aloha spirit.

Aloha!

mochi

dried pineapple slices

NUTS

HAWAIIAN TREATS
What's a day at the beach without tasty snacks? Kanani brings a gift box from her parents' sweet shop.

American Girl

Woven gift box

dried pineapple

Paddleboarding
Kanani enjoys paddling on her board. She can explore the sea coves and look for wildlife. Kanani tries to spot sea turtles and playful monk seals.

Tropical flower
print dress

'Uli'uli—
feathered
gourd rattles

Flower
lei

HULA DANCING
Kanani dances in
a Hawaiian hula costume,
including a necklace made
out of flowers, called a lei.

Kanani's
ukulele

macadamia
NUTS

McKenna
Brooks™ *2012*

McKenna is a talented gymnast, but she sometimes struggles with her schoolwork. She needs to spend a good deal of time practicing gymnastics if she wants to be successful. It's a real balancing act to keep up with school, too. But McKenna will stop at nothing to overcome a challenge.

Cooper

BEHIND THE SCENES

When author Mary Casanova was a young girl, she loved libraries and checking out books but struggled with reading comprehension. She knew firsthand what it was like to struggle in school, which helped while she was fleshing out McKenna's character.

Slip-on shoes

On the team

McKenna dreams of joining the competitive Shooting Stars gymnastics team. When she makes the team, McKenna celebrates with her goldendoodle puppy, Cooper.

McKenna

NAME
McKenna Brooks

BIRTH YEAR
2002

HOMETOWN
Seattle, Washington

BIGGEST DREAM
To overcome challenges

FAMILY
Mom, Dad,
Maisey and Mara (sisters),
Jack and Peg
(grandfather and
grandmother)

Braided pigtails

Zip-up sweatshirt

Warmed up

McKenna is ready for gymnastics practice. She wears cozy clothes over her leotard to keep warm on her way to the gym.

Cast

Stuffed panda

Stretchy bandage

GET WELL SOON

A bandage, crutches, a cast signed by her friends, and a cuddly panda help McKenna feel better quickly.

Crutches

Taking a tumble

McKenna breaks her ankle during practice. While she is injured, McKenna cannot participate in gymnastics. She spends a lot of time resting in her bedroom while she is recovering.

Necklace from her grandmother

PRACTICE BAR
McKenna and her team, the Twisters, warm up at the practice bar before competitions.

IN THE BAG
McKenna has a busy schedule. She carries everything she needs for both gymnastics and school in her sporty gym bag.

Gymnastics bag

GYMNASTICS

Shining star

McKenna works hard to overcome any challenge she is faced with. McKenna's hours of practice pay off when she shines during gymnastics competitions. Whether she takes the gold medal or not, McKenna always feels like a winner when she tries her best.

GOING FOR GOLD
McKenna practices hard and gives her best performance during a competition. She is rewarded with a golden medal!

Winning routine
McKenna loves taking part in gymnastics competitions. She hopes to one day learn a dazzling ribbon routine to perform in front of the crowds.

143

Pierced ears

Saige
Copeland™ *2013*

Saige knows that she can solve any problem with a little creativity. Even though she expresses herself best through painting, Saige speaks up when others are in need of help. Through her art and kindness, Saige aims to make the world a more beautiful place.

Saige's painting

Mimi's studio

Saige loves painting in her grandmother Mimi's art studio. Mimi's *ranchita* is an inspiring place to work. There are many things to paint, including a saddle, horses, and a stunning view of the mountains.

In the saddle

Mimi has lots of horses, and Saige loves them all. She has been riding her favorite horse, Picasso, since she was a little girl.

Picasso

Ranchita

A cowboy hat keeps the hot sun off Saige's face when she helps out at her grandmother's *ranchita*. She enjoys caring for the horses after school.

Western-style saddle

RIDING GEAR

Saige takes great care of the horses and their equipment. She always has treats ready for her animal friends.

Brush, towel, scarf, and treats

Did you know?
Mimi's horses are Spanish Barbs. The breed came to America with Spanish conquistadores, or conquerors, more than 400 years ago.

MEET
Saige

NAME
Saige Copeland

BIRTH YEAR
2003

HOMETOWN
Albuquerque, New Mexico

BIGGEST DREAM
To use her creativity to help others

FAMILY
Mom, Dad, Mimi (grandmother)

Cactus flower charm

Lend a paw

Saige likes helping others—especially animals. She spends a lot of time caring for her mischievous dog, Sam. She takes Sam for walks and trains him, too.

Sam

145

Inspired artist

In the breathtaking landscape of Albuquerque, there is inspiration everywhere. Saige loves being outside, surrounded by the beauty of nature. The best place to see everything is from the sky as she floats in her dad's hot air balloon.

TORTILLA CHIPS

ART EVERYWHERE
Saige never travels without art supplies. She can capture the beauty of the desert from here.

Pack a picnic
Saige loves the peace and quiet of the desert. A picnic with her dog, Sam, is the perfect way to enjoy a healthy meal and the view.

Envelope
(balloon)

Passenger
basket

BALLOON SET
Saige carries everything she needs
for her balloon trip—binoculars,
map, camera, and logbook—in
her red messenger bag.

Golden
cowboy boots

147

Isabelle
Palmer™ 2014

Isabelle is ready to reach for the stars when she begins her first year at a special school for the performing arts. At first, she worries that she won't be able to keep up with her classmates. When she finally learns to believe in herself, Isabelle truly becomes a star.

Pink hair extensions

Pilates straps

Dance leggings

Stretches
Keeping muscles flexible with exercise programs, such as Pilates, is important for dancers like Isabelle.

Ballet shoes

Exercise mat

Sparkly shoes

Isabelle

NAME
Isabelle Palmer

BIRTH YEAR
2005

HOMETOWN
Washington, DC

BIGGEST DREAM
To find her unique talents

FAMILY
Mom, Dad,
Jade (sister)

Ballet barre

Isabelle spends many hours at the ballet barre, perfecting her technique. She's happiest, though, when she gets to twirl and leap in the middle of the dance floor.

Dance case

Ballet bag

Isabelle carries her dance case to every ballet class. It holds all of the supplies she needs for her lessons.

Hairbands

Bun helper

Hair elastics

Name tag

TUTU

Isabelle loves snuggling up with her kitten, Tutu. But the playful kitten's claws aren't welcome around Isabelle's delicate ballet costumes!

Bobby pins

Ballet slippers

HAIR PIECE
Pink rhinestones and glitter add shimmer to Isabelle's hair when she takes the stage.

SEWING MACHINE
Isabelle and her mom sew pretty dance costumes with the help of a sewing machine.

Handmade costume

Did you know?
When ballet began in 17th century Europe, there were no tutus, leotards, or tights. Dancers performed for special events, such as weddings, in their own clothing.

MAKE A FACE
Isabelle's elegant case holds everything she needs to give her a touch of glamour on stage.

Silver ballet shoes

Sewing studio

Isabelle isn't just a star in the dance studio. Her creativity also takes a leap in her home sewing studio. Isabelle helps her mom design and make costumes for the school's Autumn Festival, and for her traveling dance troupe. Isabelle loves showing off her handmade costumes on stage.

Ballet tickets

SEWING BASKET
Isabelle keeps sewing supplies, including thread and a measuring tape, in a pink basket.

Stage fright

Isabelle loves dancing, but being in the spotlight sometimes makes her nervous. A costume made with love helps give Isabelle the confidence she needs to shine on stage.

Grace

Thomas™ 2015

Bubbly Grace is always dreaming up big ideas, like starting a new business with her best friends. No matter what problem she's up against, Grace will never give up and she always comes up with the recipe for success.

Accent braid

Charm bracelet

Pink skirt from Paris

Project Paris

Grace can't wait to go to Paris for the summer to help her aunt and uncle in their French pâtisserie. She packs lots of French-inspired outfits for her trip.

MEET
Grace

NAME
Grace Thomas

BIRTH YEAR
2005

HOMETOWN
Bentwick, Massachusetts

BIGGEST DREAM
To run her own business

FAMILY
Mom, Dad,
Josh (brother),
Grandpa and Grandma,
Bernard and Sophie
(uncle and aunt)

Sidewalk menu

Bistro style
Walking around Paris when she first arrives, Grace is amazed by all of the sidewalk bistros. She wants to try everything on the menu.

PRETTY PUPPY
While in Paris, Grace meets an adorable French bulldog. Grace takes him home and names him Bonbon.

Rolling suitcase for Paris

BEHIND THE SCENES

Starting a business is no cakewalk. Grace's author, Mary Casanova, worked closely with the director of the Jacobson Institute for Youth Entrepreneurship at the University of Iowa to make sure the aspiring baker and business owner's stories rang true.

Time to bake
Grace is so excited to help out at her aunt and uncle's pâtisserie in Paris—she loves learning all about French baking. With help, Grace whips up some tasty Parisian treats.

153

Parisian pâtisserie

Grace doesn't want her summer in Paris to come to an end. She loves spending her days baking in the pâtisserie and selling her sweet treats to customers. Bon appetit!

Pastry cart

Inspired by her summer in Paris, Grace gets to work setting up a business with her best friends—a pastry cart. Grace's family made the beautiful cart, with a pretty counter and shiny wheels, especially for her.

A bell for orders

MENU
Chocolate $ 4
Baguettes $ 2.75
Tarts $ 6

Pastry menu

Helping hand

Back home, Grace learns her grandparents' bakery may close and she is determined to stop it. Using everything she learned in Paris, Grace helps save their business.

La Pâtisserie

Shiny blue mixer

Did you know?
Pâtisseries are a type of French bakery that sell sweet pastries and baked goods. Typical items for sale include croissants, fruit tarts, macarons, and éclairs.

Mixing bowl

Open

TO-GO
Pretty boxes hold Grace's latest treats so her customers can enjoy the goodies anywhere.

PICTURE PERFECT
Grace uses elegant stands to show off her hard work. Who can resist such a lovely display?

Brazilian beach

Lea loves visiting the beach with her brother, Zac. They can swim, snorkel, and kayak. Using her underwater camera, Lea captures amazing memories to post on her travel blog.

KAYAK

This boat has a clear bottom that lets her see the beauty of the water, fish, and coral reefs below.

Removable sail

Life jacket

Kayak paddle

Snorkeling gear

MEET
Lea

NAME
Lea Clark

BIRTH YEAR
2006

HOMETOWN
St. Louis, Missouri

BIGGEST DREAM
To explore the world and help animals

FAMILY
Mom, Dad, Zac (brother)

Menu

Toucan

Flippers

Fruit stand

After a morning snorkeling, Lea visits the oceanside fruit stand for a snack. She loves sampling all of the Brazilian specialties.

Reusable tote bag

Lea
Clark™ 2016

Lea's dream is to travel the whole world. When Lea gets the chance to visit her brother in Brazil, she dives headfirst into the adventure. Lea wants to see everything in Brazil—the beaches, the exotic animals, and the rainforest. Her compass necklace leads the way!

Grandmother's compass necklace

Messenger bag

In the wild

Lea loves all animals and wants to help protect them in the wild. Lea can't believe her luck when she visits the beach at sunset and sees baby sea turtles hatching.

Did you know?
For more than 100 million years, sea turtles have lived in the world's oceans. Now, nearly all sea turtle species are endangered. Conservationists are working to protect them and their habitats.

SEA TURTLE
Lea is thrilled to spot sea turtles in the wild. They remind her of her pet turtle back home.

Lace-up sandals

157

Forest home

Lea stays with her brother and his Brazilian host family in their rainforest house. During her trip, Lea tries traditional food cooked on the Brazilian grill, and hikes into the rainforest searching for animals.

Stargazing

When night falls, Lea sits in the rainforest clearing. She looks through her telescope at all of the stars in the sky. Lea wants to record every star constellation in Brazil to compare with the night sky back home in Missouri.

SLEEP WELL
In her cozy loft bed, Lea falls asleep to the sounds of the rainforest.

Rainforest parrot

Brazilian-style grill

BEHIND THE SCENES
Author Lisa Yee had a grand adventure doing research for Lea's stories. She visited the Amazon rainforest and even met some of the local wildlife.

Loft bed

Outdoor shower

Lea's tablet

READY TO HIKE

For a hike, Lea takes her hydration backpack, walking stick, binoculars, bug spray, snacks, and rainforest butterfly guide.

Margay cat

Amazing extras

Every Girl of the Year™ comes with a range of accessories to reflect her interests and hobbies. Here are a few memorable accessories, from the first working item to the tallest.

Most pieces

GRACE'S PÂTISSERIE
In 2015, Grace's Pâtisserie was released with more than 60 play pieces. It included faux French treats, such as macarons, tarts, and cakes to play with and display.

RELEASE DATE: 2015

BAKING BITS
Bowls, baking trays, oven mitts, and more allow girls to play bake along with Grace.

Tallest

SAIGE'S HOT AIR BALLOON

RELEASE DATE: 2013

SAIGE'S HOT AIR BALLOON
Saige's hot air balloon was as big and bright as the New Mexico sky! It is the tallest product to date, standing at around 45 inches. The balloon can be deflated like a beach ball for storing and shipping.

First phone

Clock screen

RELEASE DATE: 2005

MARISOL'S FLIP PHONE
Marisol Luna™ was the first Girl of the Year to come with a pretend cell phone. It was a flip phone, which opened to reveal a working clock.

Working piece

LINDSEY'S LAPTOP
It wasn't just Lindsey who couldn't go anywhere without her laptop. Girls could use it to store 50 names and phone numbers, view the date and time, and use the calculator while they were out and about.

Laptop bag

RELEASE DATE: 2001

Smallest pet

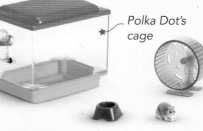

Polka Dot's cage

RELEASE DATE: 2012

MCKENNA'S HAMSTER
The smallest pet was Polka Dot, McKenna's hamster. She fit in the palm of McKenna's hand!

Smallest

SAIGE'S RING
Saige was the first to come with pierced ears and a removable ring—the smallest items in a Girl of the Year collection.

RELEASE DATE: 2013

Truly Me™

The Truly Me dolls give every girl a chance to find a best friend who is just right for her. With more than 40 dolls to choose from, and a range of eye, skin, and hair colors, girls today can express themselves through their Truly Me dolls.

Favorite things

Choosing the perfect accessories for their Truly Me dolls allows girls to show off their favorite hobbies and interests. From soccer cleats and basketballs, to tutus and guitars, there's an accessory that every girl will love.

Perfect pets

For animal-loving girls, there are plenty of super-cute pets to choose from. Whether it's a cat, dog, or horse, girls can love and care for their very own pet.

Personal style

To reflect each girl's individual personality, there are many different outfits for Truly Me dolls. Dresses, leggings, shorts, skirts, and more provide plenty of options no matter what her style.

Fashion design

At the Truly Me Signature Studio in American Girl flagship stores, girls can become instant fashion designers. They can customize an outfit for their Truly Me dolls, or get creative and design a backpack for themselves.

Dolls for every girl

Truly Me™ dolls have many different skin, hair, and eye colors—and plenty of cool hairstyles—to choose from. They encourage girls today to express themselves, discover who they truly are, and have tons of fun!

Just like me

Helping girls to embrace what makes them one of a kind, any Truly Me doll can be customized to come with no hair. These dolls make the perfect companions for girls who may be dealing with either permanent or temporary hair loss.

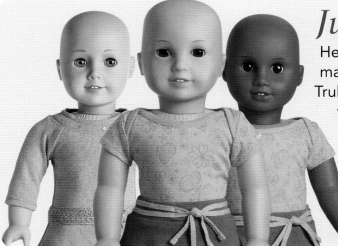

Sparkle and shine

Rings, bracelets, and earrings are just some of the beautiful accessories that allow girls to express their true style and shine both inside and out.

Hair we go!

In addition to the range of colors and styles to choose from, girls can also add extra touches. Clip-on bangs, braided headbands, and colorful highlights let each girl show off her own personal style.

Healthy start

Girls today can help look after their Truly Me dolls with special accessories. Eyeglasses and diabetes kits are just some of the things that keep modern girls healthy.

Diabetes care kit

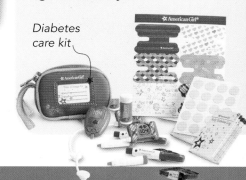

Celebrate!

Girls today have so much to celebrate—whether it's family, friendships, or a special holiday. These girls make their parties extra special with colorful outfits, delicious food, pet pals, and friends and family, of course.

Happy hearts

Pretty cards, flowers, and heart-shaped treats let girls show their friends how much they care on Valentine's Day.

Pepper
the husky

PET PARTY
Girls have fun celebrating pet birthdays with special gifts and treats.

Salon style

Girls today always shine with their own special styles. A trip to the hair salon is just the thing when girls are heading to a fancy celebration or simply trying out an exciting new look.

STYLING SET
Curly, wavy, or straight and sleek? Special tools, such as foam rollers, help girls create lots of fun new hairstyles.

Hairstyling

Girls have fun trying out new hairstyles with friends. Ponytails, crown braids, and pretty accessories, such as bows and clips, add an individual touch to any hairdo.

BRIGHT HIGHLIGHTS
Girls can express their creative styles by clipping in eye-catching hair highlights in turquoise, pink, or purple.

Styling chair

Open

SALON CAPE
A cape helps keep girls' clothes clean and dry at the salon.

BAGS OF STYLE
There is plenty of room for school supplies in this fashionable backpack.

Map of Europe

LUNCH BELL
After a busy morning, it's good to take a break! Sharing lunch with friends is the perfect way to relax.

172

School smarts

When class is in session, girls today shine as star students. Learning new things is exciting, and they always try their best. School is extra fun when friends study and work together.

SUPER SCIENCE PROJECT
Girls have fun working together to present an out-of-this-world display. The astronomy project wins first place at the science fair.

Science star

Girls love learning about the world around them. A microscope is perfect for a budding scientist to zoom in on tiny details.

Pampering

Girls today love to take time to relax after a tiring day of school and fun activities. A long, lazy soak in a bath-tub filled to the brim with bubbles washes away the cares of the day so girls can drift off to sleep with ease.

SALON STATION
Hair clips, accessories, and more are always on hand in this salon station.

Brush and style
Sometimes pets need extra special care and attention, too. A fun splash in the tub, a relaxing brush, and a pretty accessory keeps pets looking their best.

SIT BACK AND RELAX
For a special occasion, girls love visiting a spa. Spending the day being pampered is such a treat.

SOFT AND SNUG
A warm, cozy robe provides the ultimate comfort after a hot bath.

Beauty accessories

Headgear

Claw-foot bathtub

GYMNASTICS
On a beam, the floor, or the bars, girls today flip for all things gymnastics.

Basket weave braid

Jump rope

Super sports

Girls today make a great team. Their strengths really shine when they work together and have their head in the game. It's not all about winning, as long as they give it their all—and have fun, too!

GET WELL SOON
If a girl gets benched because of an injury, friends and teammates keep her spirits high.

On the field

Playing on the soccer team is a great way for girls to get outside for some fresh air and fun. Team spirit gets a boost when pom-poms and cheers get the crowd excited.

Pet pals

Pets make the perfect friends, which is why girls today hold animals close to their hearts. Whether the girls are caring for dogs, horses, or other cute creatures, they know that every pet needs their love and care.

Pomeranian puppy

Happy horses

Whether their horses are ready for a day of trail riding or settled at the stables, girls give their riding buddies all of the care and attention they deserve.

PET BED
When it's time to sleep, pets like to curl up and dream on their very own beds.

ON THE GO

Wherever a girl goes, her pet is never far behind. This collar and leash are perfect for a stylish puppy.

SERVICE DOG

Service pups offer girls a helping paw. Service training classes teach the dogs all the skills they need.

Pamper Your Pets

Pamper Your Pets

Corgi puppy

179

Fun hobbies

From dancing to roller blading or playing an instrument, girls today are always excited to try something new. Their hobbies let girls do what they love best—and have great fun with their friends, too.

Art attack

Girls today love to get creative with arts and crafts. They can express their inner artists by drawing, painting, printing, coloring, and more.

ON A ROLL
Putting on roller blades and safety gear makes for a day of outdoor fun.

Ballet barre

BALLET SHOES
Pretty ballet shoes are perfect for budding ballerinas.

CHRISTMAS SOLOS FOR T[...]

A TUNE A DAY

Violin

A☆G Violin Bow[...]

MUSIC TIME
Learning to play a musical instrument takes time and patience. But it's always fun when girls today practice with their friends.

Slumber party

It's a fun-filled night when girls gather for a super sleepover— where sleep comes second to fun with their friends. Games, dancing, snacks, and best buddies combine to create the perfect bedtime bash.

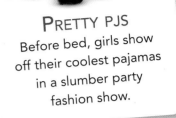

PRETTY PJS
Before bed, girls show off their coolest pajamas in a slumber party fashion show.

Pet party outfit

Terrific tunes

Every good slumber party needs music. Girls today love singing karaoke together. Even their cute furry friends get in on the act!

Pull-out bed

Board game

FUN FEAST
Girls work up big
appetites playing
board games and
having lots of fun.

Springtime

When April showers lead to May flowers, girls today happily welcome back the season's warmer weather. What could be better than spending time outdoors in gorgeous gardens or splashing in puddles with friends?

GROW TIME
A handy bench is the place to keep gardening tools, such as flower pots, a spade, and a watering can.

Beehive

Walk in the park

A park is the perfect place to enjoy the beauty of spring. On windy days, girls can watch colorful kites flying high in the bright blue sky.

Wrist guard

Knee pads

ON BOARD
Zoom into spring on a skateboard! With safety gear, including a helmet, girls are ready to go. Skateboarding is a great way to take in the sights and smells of the season.

PERFECT PICNIC
The local park is just the place for a picnic. Girls enjoy their treats while sitting in the shade.

Ice cream scoop

Bella
2013-2014

SUMMER SCOOP
An ice-cold treat is just the thing for a hot summer day.

Summertime

School is out and vacation has begun! Girls today have fun in the sun on their minds. There are so many things for best friends to do together on warm summer days.

Hit the beach

On hot days, girls head to the beach. Giggling on the sand makes for a summer day to remember. Don't forget the sunscreen!

Fall friends

With piles of vibrant leaves to jump into, ripe apples to munch, and pumpkins to pick, there is so much to do in the fall! The crisp air is perfect for hiking nature trails and pitching tents during the autumn camping season.

Outdoor party

Girls can't wait to celebrate the beauty of fall. With pumpkins from their gardens and colorful leaves from the yard, making seasonal autumn decorations is fun and easy.

Roll-up
window shade

Compass

TRAIL ACCESSORIES
When it's time to hike, girls bring everything they need, including a canteen water bottle, a compass, and binoculars for bird watching.

TRAIL MIX
Fruit & Nut

Winter fun

Cold weather can't keep girls today inside! When the temperatures drop and the snow starts to fall, the girls grab their skis, skates, and warm winter gear. It's time to head into the swirling snow for a whole lot of outdoor winter fun.

Carriage ride

Riding in a horse-drawn carriage is a magical way to admire the winter wonderland. The girls can cuddle up under cozy blankets to keep warm.

190

SKATES
Ice-skating girls can't to wait pull on a pair of white ice skates. The sparkly silver laces add a touch of winter style as girls glide across the ice.

SKI GEAR
It's time to hit the slopes with skis, boots, poles, goggles, and a helmet.

Ski goggles

Snow tube

Winter Fun!

Kwanzaa kinara

Happy Kwanzaa

Many girls celebrate Kwanzaa—
an African-American holiday that reflects
seven traditional African values, including
family, creativity, and self-improvement.
They light the seven candles in the kinara
to represent each value and the seven
days of the holiday.

HANUKKAH LIGHTS

Some girls celebrate
Hanukkah, the Jewish
Festival of Lights. They
brighten up the holiday
by lighting the candles
on the menorah.

Holiday time

Girls today celebrate many different holidays. Whatever the occasion, homemade decorations, thoughtful gifts, and festive outfits make any holiday extra fun. No matter the reason for the celebration, girls today know how to party in style!

Paper Christmas tree

Colorful ornaments

FESTIVE GIFTS
It wouldn't be the holidays without giving friends special gifts, like this glittery snowglobe.

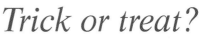

Trick or treat?
On Halloween, girls put on their favorite costumes. Whether they're dressed up in something sweet, funny, or scary, girls are ready for trick-or-treating. Even their super-adorable pets join in the fun!

Meet the team

It takes a big team of talented people to make a character perfect. Go behind the scenes to find out about just a few of the people who bring the American Girl® dolls and their stories to life.

★★★★★★★★★★
Name: Jennifer
Job: Editor

As a girl, my favorite thing was reading and writing stories. It still is, which is why I love working as an editor. I got to choose the authors and help write the stories for Julie, Rebecca, Kanani, and Maryellen. They're almost like daughters to me! I grew up near San Francisco in the 1970s, so I especially relate to Julie's story.

★★★★★★★★★★
Name: Steve
Job: Product Designer

As a designer, it's my job to come up with exciting new product ideas for American Girl. Sometimes, I build full-scale models of new toy ideas to make sure they are just right before they are made. There is something magical about seeing a girl play with a toy I designed—that's the best part of my job. My favorite doll is Kit because she was introduced the same year I started working for American Girl.

Steve works on an original full-scale model of the Seaside Diner from Maryellen's collection.

★★★★★★★★★★★

Name: Mark
Job: Historian

I work together with authors, editors, and product designers to help bring each character's story to life. My job is to make sure the BeForever™ characters' worlds are as true to the past as possible. I make sure every product and part of a character's story is historically correct by reading books and old newspapers and magazines and touring museums. My favorite character right now is Melody. I love her compelling stories.

★★★★★★★★★★★★

Name: Meagan
Job: Research Librarian

I collect and manage library resources, and conduct research that inspires and informs the development of toys and books for American Girl. The best part of my job is helping people find the right piece of information that answers a question, solves a problem, or inspires an idea. I am also lucky to work with smart, creative people every day. I like Kaya because I love nature and animals, and her story of bravery inspires me to be courageous.

★★★★★★★

Name: Wendy
Job: Art Director

My job combines all of the things that I am passionate about: Design, history, and reading. I work with editors, photographers, illustrators, and historians to make the American Girl characters come to life visually. My favorite American Girl doll is Josefina. Her artistic nature and the vibrant color palette of New Mexico are so inspiring to me as a creative designer.

Glossary

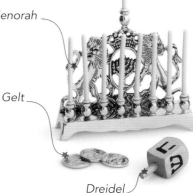

Menorah

Gelt

Dreidel

American Civil War
A war between the northern and southern states of the United States, which took place between 1861 and 1865.

American Revolution
Between 1775 and 1783, 13 British colonies in North America fought against British rule. This revolution led to the formation of the United States of America.

Cenote (se-NO-tay)
A natural swimming hole formed by collapsed rock. They are common in parts of Mexico and were used as a water source by the Mayans.

Chinese New Year
A festival celebrated at the start of a new year according to the Chinese calendar, typically in February.

Civil rights movement
A campaign during the 1950s and 1960s that fought for equal rights for African-Americans.

Cradleboard
A baby carrier made with a wooden frame, hides, and woven grasses or reeds. Cradleboards were typically decorated with paint, quills, beads, or shells.

Dreidel
A pointed, four-sided spinning top used for a game played during Hanukkah.

Melody joins the fight for equal rights.

Gelt
Money, or chocolate coins, given to children during Hanukkah.

Great Depression
A time during the 1930s when the United States' economy collapsed. Millions of people were left out of work and lost their homes.

Hanukkah
A Jewish holiday, also known as the Festival of Lights. A celebration of a miracle from Jewish history, it is typically celebrated in December.

Immigrant
A person who moves to another country to live and work.

Kwanzaa
An African-American holiday lasting seven days, first celebrated in December 1966. Kwanzaa honors seven traditional African values.

Longhouse
A permanent structure of poles covered with tule mats and hides. It is built by Native Americans for shelter over the winter or long-term living.

Loom
A device used to weave thread or yarn into cloth.

Mayans
The people who lived throughout many parts of Central America over 3,000 years ago.

Menorah
A nine-candle holder, used during Hanukkah. One candle is lit for each day of the eight-day holiday—the ninth candle is used to light all other candles.

Mexican War of Independence
A war between 1810 and 1821, during which Mexico fought to become independent from Spanish rule.

New World
A name for South, Central, and North America given by European explorers in the 1500s.

Nez Perce
The Nez Perce, or Niimíipu, are a Native American tribe who live in the Pacific Northwest region of the United States.

Pâtisserie (pa-TIH-ser-ree)
A special type of bakery in France and Belgium that sells pastries and cakes.

Pioneers
People who are among the first to move and settle in a new country.

Pow-wow
A celebration in Native American culture with dancing, singing, food, and traditional arts and crafts.

Rancho
A ranch or area of land where families would live, grow crops, and graze animals.

Ration book
A book with coupons for food, clothes, and other restricted items used during World War II, and the years following, in the United Kingdom.

Rebozo
An item of clothing, similar to a shawl, worn by girls and women in Mexico.

Riding habit
A tailored jacket, shirt, long skirt, hat, and boots worn by women for horseback riding from the mid-1600s.

Sabbath
A day of rest and worship, observed in Judaism from Friday evening to Saturday evening.

Service dog
A type of assistance dog specially trained to help people with a range of disabilities.

Skiff
A small, light boat, either with oars or a sail, usually for one person.

Slavery
When someone legally owns another person, controlling where they live, and forcing them to work without pay.

Tepee
A cone-shaped tent, traditionally built by Native Americans using animal hides, mats, and wooden poles.

Travois (tra-VWAH)
A wooden frame attached to an animal, such as a horse or dog, for pulling heavy loads.

War of 1812
A war over trade, independence, and land, between the United States of America and the United Kingdom.

World War II
A global war that took place between 1939 and 1945. It was fought between the Axis powers (Germany, Japan, and Italy) and the Allies (Britain, Canada, the US, and the Soviet Union, along with other countries). It affected the whole world and millions of people were killed.

Service dog

197

Index

Main entries are in **bold**

Felicity's hat

Lanie's bracelet

Josefina's fan and shawl

Melody's radio

Molly's instruments

Julie's tie-dye bag

McKenna's gymnastics medal

Grace's apron

Samantha's doll

Isabelle's tiara

Kit's telephone

ACKNOWLEDGMENTS

Senior Editor Tori Kosara
Project Editor Eleanor Rose
Senior Designer Lisa Sodeau
Additional Design Sam Bartlett and Nathan Martin
Pre-Production Producer Siu Yin Chan
Senior Producer Louise Daly
Managing Editor Paula Regan
Design Manager Guy Harvey
Publisher Julie Ferris
Art Director Lisa Lanzarini
Publishing Director Simon Beecroft

First American Edition, 2016
Published in the United States by DK Publishing
345 Hudson Street, New York, NY 10014

Page design copyright © 2016 Dorling Kindersley Limited
DK, a division of Penguin Random House LLC
16 17 18 19 10 9 8 7 6 5 4 3 2 1
001–283062–Sep/16

A catalog record for this book
is available from the
Library of Congress.

ISBN: 978-1-4654-4496-7

DK books are available at special discounts when
purchased in bulk for sales promotions, premium,
fund-raising, or educational use. For details, contact:
DK Publishing Special Markets, 345 Hudson Street,
New York, NY 10014
SpecialSales@dk.com

Printed and bound in China

www.americangirl.com
www.dk.com

A WORLD OF IDEAS:
SEE ALL THERE IS TO KNOW

DK would like to thank Alex Belmonte, Kate Carlyle,
Dave Conant, Andrea Debbink, Jodi Goldberg,
Virginia Gunderson, Sara Hereley, Julie Parks,
Nancy Price, Isa Primavera, Mark Speltz, Barbara
Stretchberry, Jessica Wells, and Riley Wilkinson at
American Girl; Charnita Belcher and Ryan Ferguson
at Mattel; Valerie Tripp for writing the foreword;
and Pleasant T. Rowland.

Thanks also to Hannah Dolan, Rosie Peet, and Allie
Singer for extra editorial help; Marcel Carry and
Rhys Thomas for design assistance; Laura
Palosuo for proofreading; and Helen Peters
for writing the index.